There Is Always
a Choice

There Is Always a Choice

Allegories for Living

María Elena Pellinen

DEDICATION

To my sister Tere.

One day, my sister Tere gave me a whole ten years to write a book.
Since that day several decades have gone by, but Tere never lost hope.
Because of her enthusiasm and belief in me,
this book of philosophical allegories is dedicated to her and the
twenty thousand plus one students who have crossed my path.
Because there is always a choice.

ACKNOWLEDGMENT

My deepest gratitude goes to Dr. Peter Koestenbaum, my professor, mentor, and friend from whom I received the necessary tools to help me apply the classical philosophies in logical, therapeutic, and practical ways.

I am also very grateful to my daughter, Dr. Teresa Delfín, for her comments, and to my editor and friend, Byron Tidwell, whose timely and artistic strokes have contributed immensely toward a better view of this philosophical landscape.

CONTENTS

1

So Far, So Good!

"LIFE IS PHILOSOPHY and philosophy is life." The professor stood next to her lectern in front of her new students on their first day of class. Some stared back blankly, some gazed out the windows, a few in the front row of desks listened with close attention, and three scattered students yawned almost in unison.

"For our first class exercise each of you will pronounce my name as *clearly* and *distinctly* as possible." She continued, "My name is Lucia, just like the beautiful love song Santa Lucia by Miguel Rios." No sign of recognition from a single student. "No?" she said, when all of the sudden, an elderly woman started to hum its melody. "That is the one," Lucia said. "Now, let's all of us at the same time pronounce my name: Lu-SEE-a. If you pronounce my name in Spanish the way it is supposed to be pronounced, you can't help but smile. One more time everybody," and everyone in unison said, "Lucia."

Lucia resumed, "Now your second bit of information: you will find we are all capable of more than we may realize. For example, I myself am capable of wearing two hats and one sombrero." One by one, students began to direct their attention to Lucia. It was not a sudden change, more like a slow-moving wave. Lucia's humor, energy, and enthusiasm proved infectious. A sly smile revealed Lucia expected this.

"One of my three hats represents my philosophy class, the other hat represents my humanities class, and the sombrero represents my Spanish class." She arched an eyebrow. "And if you haven't enrolled in humanities or Spanish, I expect to see you next semester."

Though she had lived in the United States for decades, Lucia grew up in her native country of Mexico. In high school she studied logic, ethics, and history of philosophy, subjects not usually studied in American high schools. Lucia's high school in Mexico followed the European model of education and included far more esoteric classes. Among those subjects, she fell absolutely and completely in love with her philosophy class. There she learned that her great uncle Ezequiel A. Chávez, a philosophy professor, writer, and educator at the turn of the century, had been professor for her high school ethics teacher. Just like her great uncle, Lucia fell head over heels with philosophy.

While a student of philosophy at the University of Guadalajara during the 1960s, a local high school hired Lucia to teach ethics and logic. Considering the years of education required to teach far less sophisticated subjects in American high schools, it may be considered unusual to have just graduated high school in Mexico City and begin teaching that same year while simultaneously attending university classes. How could she do that without a teaching credential? "Well, my friend," Lucia told many friends and students, "for logic class, I taught Aristotelian logic and . . ." She said slyly, with a twinkle in her eyes, "I repeated the very same symbolic logic lectures I heard in my university classes." She chuckled, "It was the 1960s, and Mexico was a third world country. I spoke well, dressed respectably, and had a clean face. What more did I need?

"During those days," Lucia mused, "I lived philosophy 24-7 as either a student or a teacher. Never mind I had no time for fun, movies, dances, or even dates! I dedicated all my time to teaching and studying, and let me tell you, that lifestyle never caused me stress, anxiety, or concern because philosophy entertained me full-time. And, possibly most importantly, my friend, I learned from Hegel that 'nothing is ever accomplished without enthusiasm.' For me, I am never short of enthusiasm."

In Guadalajara, Lucia taught high school mornings and attended college classes afternoons and evenings. One single graduation requirement eluded her: the ability to speak, understand, and write in a foreign language. Lucia's older sister, who lived in the United States, invited Lucia to come and live with her and immerse herself in the English language. Once she gained the knowledge and understanding of American English, she would return to Mexico to finish her degree. But moving away from the safety of home and loving and caring parents was daunting. Her father told her, "Dear Lucia, if your sister invites you to go to the United States, go! The United States is the number one country in the world. Besides, as the Good Book says, 'A prophet is not without honor, except in his own country.'" With that paternal and biblical advice in mind, Lucia came to the United States.

Lucia recounted her story to her students, going—in their eyes—from aloof faculty to a real person with accomplishments and challenges. She told her students, "At the beginning of this lecture, I said I would be your favorite teacher. That was a bit of hyperbole. I do want us to be friends, possibly even best friends. We will use the Socratic method in my class, and that virtually requires us to be friends. Even when I meet someone, however briefly, I want him or her to be my best friend, even if for only a few moments. Those sixty seconds that I may spend with that person I may just have met are, at that precise moment, my most meaningful sixty seconds. Besides, you never know if those few seconds may transcend themselves toward a lifetime of friendship."

At the end of class, several students gathered at the front of the classroom and made a hasty exit. One of the other students, a young woman named Glynis stepped forward assertively, extending her hand.

Lucia took her hand, smiling, and thanked her for enrolling in her class. Glynis said, "So far, so good, Professor!"

Without batting an eye, the professor responded, "Call me, Lucia."

So far so good.

2

The Second Class,
the First Class

"**B**UENOS DÍAS!" LUCIA strode into the classroom. Three students, all of Hispanic ancestry, mumbled "Buenos días" in sullen response. Most of the other, English-speaking students simply looked like deer in headlights.

Removing books from her bag and placing them on her desk, Lucia counted, "I see one, two, three, four . . . six new faces. You missed my first class. Check with a fellow student about the subject matter. It is very important. There will be a test."

Lucia brooked no formality. Far from remaining behind a desk or podium, she was in almost constant movement in and among the class. She continued, "For those of you who might have missed my first class, do not worry about it since the only thing you missed was one hour of my accent." Several of the new students breathed audible relief. "Your first class is truly today."

Moving to the front of the classroom, Lucia leaned on her desk. "Allow me to introduce our guest of honor in today's lecture." Wary, everyone glanced nervously around the room. From the assertion in the first class meeting when Lucia pledged to be their favorite teacher, her students knew Lucia was no ordinary instructor, and for all they knew, this "guest of honor" was one of them, and any one might be suddenly called upon. "I see you looking to your left and to your right for our special guest. But don't look for Him. Just allow His Essence to perceive you! There is nothing more magnificent then being perceived by the Almighty. As the Irish Bishop and philosopher George Berkeley said, "To be is to be perceived."

No one understood Lucia's statement of "Berkeley's information." No one dared ask a question.

Lucia said, "I hope all of you are willing to put in practice my most difficult requirement for this class." She looked over her deathly silent classroom. What could this difficult requirement be? Every single student tensed, doubting whether they could achieve it.

"The requirement is *ignorance*," Lucia said, with her big smile. Silence. Then chuckles of relief. All relaxed.

Thus, with every one feeling at home, Lucia began the first philosophy class.

3

The Four Rights and the Four Wrongs

LUCIA STOOD BEFORE the class, tall and commanding. Every eye was upon her. Every student waited in anticipation. She turned her gaze to the row of windows overlooking the wide lawn outside the classroom. "Can we agree it is a beautiful day outside?" she asked.

Her students nodded and mumbled assents.

"So, we are agreed?" Lucia confirmed. "We are nearing the end of summer and just beginning to feel the autumn season. The sky is nearly clear with only a few high clouds. The sun shines brightly. A gentle southerly breeze ruffles the leaves, and the temperature is warm and comfortable. Who would like to skip this class and go outside and enjoy the day?"

One hand raised tentatively, followed by another. "Come on," Lucia urged, "be truthful." More hands went up until finally every student had a hand in the air. "Very good." Lucia smiled. "Outside we go."

The class settled under a broad shade tree. Some sat, some reclined. Lucia leaned against the tree. "We just need one more thing," she said. "We need one of you to volunteer to take highly detailed notes to share with everyone else. Who will do that?"

No hand rose. A girl in a striped shirt asked, "What would I get if I take notes for everybody?"

"Excellent question. The class now begins."

"Today, we are going to learn Aristotle's concept of *magnanimity*. Does any one of you have a magnanimous friend?" And when no one responded, she said, "Well, I have and her name is Mary. Mary is the mother of three very different girls and a very spoiled husband. Somehow, Mary is always capable of keeping everyone being nice to each other and never loses her self-control. This is why I have nicknamed her Mary the Magnanimous!"

The girl who asked the last question raised her hand again. "Professor, may I ask a question?"

"Please do," Lucia replied gently, moving near her.

"It sounds like your friend is kind of weak minded and appeasing to her daughters and no-good husband. How can you admire such a doormat?"

All heads turned toward Lucia, anticipating a rebuke. She considered. "I think the descriptive term for the husband was spoiled, which is different from 'no-good.' Doormat? Hmmm. I don't believe anyone who actually knows Mary would ever consider her a doormat. Let me try to provide some additional information that may allow you to have a different insight. Who is familiar with the philosopher Aristotle?"

Her question received blank looks from most of the students.

A student near the front tentatively raised his hand. "I think he was in that Oliver Stone movie about Alexander, that Roman dude?"

"Alexander the Great was Greek. Same general area," Lucia added.

"Yeah," the student went on, "that guy you said. I think he was, like, the old dude who was, like, his teacher or something?"

"Was that the one with Angelina Jolie?" another student asked. The first student gave him a thumbs-up.

Interrupting the digression, Lucia said, "Yes, Aristotle was Alexander the Great's tutor. Aristotle knew and wrote about many things. He was first a scientist thanks to his father, Nicomachus. Aristotle learned from his father that virtually all processes have a *cause-effect relationship.* With that in mind, to be *magnanimous* means to follow his ethical formula of *the four rights.* That is to say, one must always do (1) the right thing, (2) at the right time, (3) in the right place, and (4) for the right reason."

Lucia repeated the four points again. She waited a moment for her students to absorb the ideas. Continuing, she said, "Keep in mind that for Aristotle there are human choices that are never right, like committing a crime, adultery, stealing, abusing people, etcetera, because these choices are always wrong.

"Let me throw another name at you: John Locke. He was an English philosopher and physician of the seventeenth century, widely regarded as one of the most influential of Enlightenment thinkers. Read about him in your textbook. John Locke would have said that we are not born *magnanimous*, we are born babies." The students chuckled at the joke. Lucia continued, "But we can become *magnanimous* just like my friend Mary. Mary somehow knows how to balance the needs of all her family, like those of her elderly mother-in-law, those of her very spoiled husband, and those of her three very different and independent daughters. I met Mary after her daughter number one, Danielle, became my student.

"During Danielle's first class, she said to me, 'I must warn you that I don't know how to read.'"

Don't know how to read? I thought, *This is unusual: making it all the way into college without the ability to read.* "So, I said to Danielle, 'That is no problem as long as you don't have a problem with my accent and you can understand me.' And Danielle said to me, 'That is no problem, I understand you fine, and as a matter of fact, I find your accent rather charming.'

"'Well,' I said to Danielle, 'I am rather curious now. Can you read a little or not at all?' Danielle said she could read a little. So, I opened Plato's *Republic*, my choice of book for that class, to a random page, and the young lady began to read out loud. She read very well, with no pauses, hesitations, or difficulties with any of the words. But I wondered about her comprehension. I asked her to tell me in her own words what she had just read.

Danielle quickly observed, 'I believe Plato did not want any "civil strife" among the citizens of his ideal state because brothers do not fight against brothers.' She snapped my book close and gave it to me, smiling a big smile. She said, 'Wait till I tell my sisters about this!' I said, 'Danielle, from my point of view, you have no problems reading whatsoever.'

"'Really?' she said. I don't think she quite believed me yet. Danielle said, 'Do you know that since I was in second grade, I was told that I could not read? That's what my teachers wrote on my report cards: Danielle has difficulty with reading. It made me always believe reading was something I couldn't do well. That's what I always thought during summer vacations when I laid out next to the pool and read books by Jane Austen and Louisa May Alcott and the Bronte sisters. All the time I read, I thought I had difficulty reading.' Then Danielle thanked me for my encouraging words.

Frankly speaking, I had no idea what I had done for Danielle, but she looked happy. By the way, Danielle finished that class with an A plus. Thus, Danielle's story illustrates very well the danger of what the nineteenth-century Danish philosopher Søren Kierkegaard calls *psychological burden.* Imagine spending twelve years of your life believing that you are a loser. And some poor people actually spend their entire life never knowing how to find *psychic energy*—the very same energy that transformed my student as she got rid of all of those years of that *psychological burden.* Within time, Danielle became my very good friend, and now she is a very happy schoolteacher while Mary continues being my *magnanimous* friend, always capable of balancing the four rights, *with the right daughters,* in the *right place,* and *for the right reason,* through her entire life."

Lucia scanned the sea of blank faces in the class before her. She said, "Perhaps my story of my friend Mary's magnanimity is obscured by her daughter Danielle's accomplishment. Allow me to tell give another example of a magnanimous choice.

"A few years ago I got to know the oldest daughter of the family, a young and playful girl who just graduated from high school and was beginning classes at community college. Her name was Jennifer, and Jennifer and I became great friends. In her first quarter at college, Jennifer started dating a man named Brad. Let me tell you, *that* was a bone of contention in her house because Jennifer just turned eighteen, and Brad was close to thirty-five. Still, they seemed a good match, and Jennifer's parents saw a lot of good in Brad. By spring quarter, Brad convinced Jennifer to move with him. Her parents weren't immediately happy, but they did not want to stand between Jennifer and her happiness. Jennifer and Brad spent an idyllic summer, but before fall quarter began, Jennifer was pregnant.

"Her young friends encouraged her to have an abortion. They said, 'You're too young to be held back by a baby,' and all the other things young people say to each other when a girl gets pregnant unexpectedly. However, Jennifer was convinced that abortion would never be a choice for her.

"After her firm decision to have the baby, Brad asked Jennifer to marry him. This was the first time Jennifer realized she must confront many choices in addition to her decision to keep the baby. Over the five months they lived together, Jennifer was disappointed to learn that

Brad's choices of music were very different from hers. So were his choices of movies and sports and clothes. He liked to go out alone with his friends a couple of nights every week, leaving her to sit home by herself. He found her friends immature, and she found his friends old and boring. Still, Jennifer was happy to know that she was going to be a mom. She resigned herself to accept the marriage proposal so her baby would have a dad.

Two years later, Jennifer got pregnant again. Even with the growing differences between her and Brad, Jennifer was glad to know her baby boy would have a sibling.

"As she could, Jennifer kept going to college and working toward her degree. In a social sciences class, Jennifer met a young man named Ivan. Ivan's birthday came six days ahead of Jennifer's. When they celebrated together over coffee inside the Student Union, they laughed to find they were virtually the same age. They shared their life stories and found they had much in common. Ivan understood the problems related to her married life, and she understood his dreams and goals. They became by day the best of friends so much so that friendship soon became love.

"Jennifer screwed her courage to the sticking place and sat down with Brad one night after the children went to bed and the house was dim and quiet. To her immense relief, Brad confessed his extreme frustration as well. Brad said as much as he loved her—and he did love her—he realized their relationship was wrong for both of them and would only become more frustrating. Jennifer and Brad agreed to a friendly divorce while the children were still so young.

"It wasn't long before the children got accustomed to seeing Ivan in their house at the same time that Brad came to take the children with him and when he brought them back. I must tell you that these three adults got along very well, and the children felt surrounded with a very friendly and warm family ambiance.

"This may surprise you. I know it surprised me. A few weeks ago, I heard from Jennifer that she and Ivan will be married in December. Jennifer's children are now four and six years old. She came up with a plan to help her kids accept that Mom has a new husband. Jennifer asked Brad to obtain a license so he can be the one performing the marriage ceremony in front of his children. I found that creative and magnanimous on Jennifer's part: to understand and care for her children's perceptions with sensitivity and to retain Brad as an integral part of her life by asking him to 'oversee' this significant transition while continuing as their children's father. And, for Ivan to agree and be comfortable with this ceremony is magnanimous on his part.

"Brad agreed to perform this role as the licensed minister on behalf of his children. Sure, he feels occasional twinges of doubt and regret, but he is able to set those feelings aside for everyone's greater good. The choice of doing the right thing in the right place at the right time for the right reason is what Aristotle calls a 'magnanimous' choice.

"In other words, the *four rights* have to be put in practice time and again. As Aristotle said in talking about ethics, "One sunny day or one bird in the sky does not mean that spring time has arrived."

The girl in the striped shirt raised her hand, and Lucia nodded. The girl asked, "Professor Lucia, at the beginning of class when you asked for someone to take notes so everybody else could go out and enjoy the nice day, were you looking for somebody to be magnanimous?"

"*Exactamente*, my observant student!" Lucia crowed. "Full marks and a gold star for you today!"

With long shadows extending from the school buildings in the golden glow of sunset, Lucia ended the class. Students clambered up from the grass and wandered off in many directions. Glynis, the girl that made the aggressive approach on the first day, again came first in line to see Lucia following class.

Accustomed to such students, Lucia put no barrier between them. Lucia"What did you think of today's class?" she asked Glynis.

Glynis replied, "There's a lot to absorb." She bit her lip and looked imploringly into Lucia's eyes. "I will be thinking of everything we covered and reading the next several chapters in the text book." She smiled broadly in relief, having said her piece.

"Good job," Lucia said, patting her hand.

Another student, a man quite a bit older than usual first-year students, approached. Lucia asked, "Joel, did you get anything from today's class?"

"You know my name?" Joel reacted. His heavy eyebrows and dark circles under his eyes gave the appearance of a dour attitude. His voice though was warm and friendly. "I mean, if you had your seating chart, I could see that. But out here, that's kind of random."

"Why shouldn't I know your name?" Lucia countered. "You know my name. Isn't it common decency and respect for me to know yours?" She gathered her papers and books and stuffed them into her bag.

"I don't want to hold you up," Joel told her. "May I walk you to your car and ask questions along the way?"

Lucia responded, "Of course you can. And Glynis can come along too."

They strolled across the tree-shaded lawn toward staff parking. "You know, Professor," Joel said, "thanks to your lecture, I am very seriously considering majoring in philosophy." They paused for some cars to pass in the driveway between the class building and the parking lot.

"Well, my friend"—Lucia smiled—"nothing pleases me more than to hear that."

"So, Professor, may I ask a philosophical question related to the class topic?" Joel became serious, and the pitch of his voice lowered. Lucia paused to give him her full attention. He continued, "Would Aristotle consider it a *magnanimous choice* to be able to meet the right woman at the right time in the right bed for the right reason?"

Lucia's eyes narrowed ever so slightly. "And are these two people single?" she asked.

Joel hesitated. "One is and the other is not."

"Then, the answer is *never*, my friend," Lucia answered firmly. Very firmly.

"But isn't being magnanimous being the bigger person given the situation?" Joel insisted.

"That's not necessarily big of you. That's *bigamy*," Lucia responded.

"But if no one found out, and it didn't hurt anybody—"

Lucia cut off the discussion. "I'll tell what, my friend. Why don't you bring up the subject again during our next class since right now, it is rather late and I need to get home to the right family?"

With a strained smile, Joel hurried off to his car.

At the next class meeting, Lucia watched the hands of the big clock at the head of the room tick five minutes past start time. No Joel. She began class. At the end of class, she waited ten minutes in case Joel stopped by. That afternoon, Lucia received Joel's withdrawal slip in interoffice mail. She always regretted losing students.

4

Caloric Joy

FOR A MOMENT, Lucia and Dr. Fisher, department chair, paused in the social sciences building hallway, at an impasse in discussion of Carl Jung's collective unconsciousness. Fisher's aide hurried by, and Lucia commented, "Kaneesha parted her hair on the right today."

Dr. Fisher looked Kaneesha's direction. "I didn't notice that. But then, you are keen on observations."

"So what's with keeping your left hand in your pocket?" Lucia asked bluntly.

"Not for public consumption," Fisher answered. "Stop by next Wednesday and tell me how your new intro students are getting on." Fisher abruptly left and strode away without looking back.

A bit later, Lucia stopped by the pharmacy and almost collided with a pleasantly plump woman. "Alice!" Lucia exclaimed. "I am so happy to see you, and even more happy as I see your radiant aura of joy."

Astonished and blushing, Alice placed her hand on her cheek. "It's that obvious, is it?" She threw her arms around Lucia in happy embrace. "You're right! I am so very, very happy!"

"From the look of you, I think you and your new husband have been enjoying great meals." Lucia smiled.

"Oh, my god, you are so right!" Alice laughed. "I *am* eating and celebrating and showing my extra happy pounds. You know, I lost so much weight when my first husband died and all of a sudden found myself a widow with six children." Alice turned a small circle, showing off her zaftig figure. "But, look at me now with a new dad for my kids, and me now a new mom for his four kids. We are one big happy family." Alice hugged Lucia and gave her a light kiss on her cheek. "Thank you, Lucia, for noticing my extra caloric joy."

"And there is always a choice. Isn't there?"

The pharmacy checkout clerk whispered to her customer, "I have never met anyone other than Lucia who gets away with those kind of comments."

5

Moral and Intellectual Virtues

A T THE EDGE of the park, Lucia broke into a happy skip, rapidly putting distance between herself and her family. Her ten-year-old twins, Laura and Ellen, exchanged startled glances and hurried to join her. "Mom!" her teenage son Sam called, embarrassed, "C'mon! Act your age!"

Lucia's husband Gary placed a calming hand on Sam's shoulder. "Not a good idea to tell your mother to act her age," he cautioned. "I learned that a long time ago."

Suddenly the twins turned around and galloped back. "Mommy's going to her philosophy bench," Ellen announced.

"She said we should entertain ourselves," Laura added.

"So, what do you want to do?" Gary asked. *It's Sunday*, he thought. He expected this.

"Can we go to the Ocho for ice cream?" Sam asked.

Gary looked at his round-faced son's ever-rounding middle. "Yeah, why not? We'll see your mother when she gets home."

On every good weather Sunday, Lucia came to the big park and sat on the bench beneath the gnarled old oak on the west side, which provided all-day shade during the warm months. This place was her private practice, where students would find her for ad hoc tutoring and where friends dropped by for free philosophical advice. Under the deep blue and almost cloudless sky, Lucia happily sat and watched couples, singles, and groups stroll by basking in the day's warmth. She tilted her face up to enjoy the sun's warmth, filtered through the dense canopy.

"Lucia, it is so good to see you!" A former student, Cathy, stood close, waiting for Lucia to invite her to sit.

Still in her reverie, Lucia said, "Good morning, my dear. How are you?"

"Very well, Lucia, but . . ." The girl hesitated. She looked away, hoping for a clear escape route.

"But what, Cathy?" Lucia asked gently.

Mortified, Cathy blurted, "Lucia, please help me. I don't know that to do with my little boy!"

Caught by surprise by the passion of Cathy's remark, Lucia removed her sunglasses and patted the seat next to her. "Come sit," she said. Cathy settled next to her, and Lucia adjusted to give Cathy her full attention. "First, tell me how old he is."

"Bobby is four."

"And what is his problem?"

"Oh dear, Professor!" Cathy cried, "Bobby is disobedient, capricious, and he's a little liar. Nothing I do works. I try time-outs. I lecture. I don't believe in spanking, but I'm ready to try that. Do you think that I should put him in preschool to straighten him out?"

"He's four?" Lucia considered. "My goodness, Cathy, you have already wasted the last four years!"

Cathy's eyes filled with tears. "Tell me what to do," Cathy begged.

Seeing Cathy's expression grow dour, Lucia realized she may have been too blunt with her former student. She patted Cathy's arm gently, consoling her. "You see, Cathy," Lucia said softly. "An infant's brain is a little sponge: it absorbs everything that he experiences. If we wait until he is older to correct his mistakes, we risk robbing him of moral virtues and, perhaps, even *instilling* in him bad vices."

Even more aghast, Cathy exclaimed, "Do you mean that I have already robbed him of his moral virtue?"

Lucia grasped Cathy's hand. In flight reflex, Cathy had begun to bolt. "Relax, my dear. You have asked a very good question, and I will answer you. Remember Aristotle?" Cathy nodded, wide-eyed. "Well," Lucia continued, "consider what Aristotle, one of my favorite philosophers, said, 'Virtue is the excellence that improves human quality'."

Cathy frowned, uncomprehending. Lucia elaborated, "Just as glasses improve our eyesight, virtue improves our human conduct. You see, justice is a virtue, and injustice is a vice. Is this clear so far, Cathy?

"No, not really. This is a little confusing."

"Consider this," Lucia continued, "what if every parent took their children to kindergarten in the hope that the teacher will teach their child discipline? If a teacher has a classroom of twenty children, all of whom she must teach discipline, how can she teach ABCs and shapes and maybe a little one plus one equals two? Can you not see the teacher facing utter chaos?" Wide-eyed, Cathy nodded. "Now then, what was it you first asked me? Ah, yes: 'Do you think that I should put him in preschool to straighten him out?'" Cathy blushed. Lucia added gently, "So you agree this is not the obligation of the teacher? Aristotle says the teacher is one who inculcates scholastic education in the minds of the little one. That is to say, a teacher should inspire *intellectual* virtues, and the obligation of the parent is to instill *moral* virtues."

The light of insight broke through. Cathy grasped the idea.

"I have a question," Lucia said. "I know you have observed the behavior of children varies from one family to another. Why are there those families who teach their children very well whereas others lose total control and fill their lives with disasters and misunderstandings?" She paused a brief moment, not expecting a reply.

"The questions that you ask me today," Lucia continued, "are questions of the ages. Even Plato and Aristotle, Greek philosophers born three hundred years before Christ, asked these same questions. In fact, Aristotle, whom I think we can agree was expert in human conduct and a professor of ethics, logic, physics, and metaphysics, had already deeply analyzed different conducts: conduct that is guided by virtue and conduct that is, unfortunately, guided by vice. Let's sit back a moment and take deep breaths and enjoy this wonderful weather."

Teacher and student scanned the panorama of the broad park with its deep green grass and expanse bordered by big leafy oak and ash trees and the near cloudless skies and the couples holding hands and the joggers and skaters zipping by and the children playing with unrestrained joy. The two shared a moment of peace.

Resuming, the professor began, "So we learn from Aristotle about intellectual and moral virtues. As parents we have the obligation to instill in our children these two qualities. Our task is to teach the importance of the civic and social obligation of education, insisting that they always complete their homework and never are absent or late.

Parents also have the obligation and responsibility to demand and require respect and to help the child understand the value of moral duty. Their child should be obedient and responsible with no alternatives given to the child."

"That is very hard," Cathy said.

"Of course it is hard. Who said being a parent is easy? My dear Cathy, although the first four years have already gone by, there is still time to ensure that these moral lessons are fulfilled. Since you have been thinking of this to the point that you sought me out for advice, I know you will apply yourself and teach your son moral values and you will succeed."

A flamboyantly dressed passing skater caught their attention briefly. They watched him glide by, his multicolored streamers billowing behind him in the breeze. They laughed aloud. Lucia asked, "So why did you believe you would find me here in the park?"

"Aren't you always here?" Cathy asked, puzzled. "That's what everybody says."

A trifle embarrassed, Lucia chuckled. "Well then, Cathy, perhaps you will allow me to enjoy the beautiful day and wander in my thoughts. Say 'hello' to your family for me."

Cathy brushed herself off. "Thank you for listening. And thanks for your advice. I will take it to heart."

"You do what you can do," Lucia mused.

"Professor, next weekend if you have the time, would you come to my house for dinner? I seem to recall you saying paella is one of your favorite dishes. I would love to prepare it for you by way of thanks." Cathy appeared wide-eyed and hopeful.

"Ah, the mention of it makes me hungry," Lucia smiled. "I'll be there."

"Will seven o'clock Friday a week from next work for you?" Lucia quickly accepted. "Well, good then," Cathy gushed, excited in anticipation of this important visitor. "I'll see you then. Good-bye, Professor, and thank you very much again."

"Don't mention it, Cathy, don't mention it," Lucia said, "and keep a firm hand on that boy of yours. Don't allow him to give you too much trouble."

"Not anymore," Cathy replied with a lift in her voice that reflected the hope and sense of joy she had in her heart.

Watching Cathy stroll away with a refreshed swing in her step, Lucia settled back on her park bench and dug into her satchel, searching among the other books for the one to read.

6

Stress

A S LUCIA SAT on her bench reading, a light breeze caressed her face. She thoroughly enjoyed delving into her new book, *The Care of the Soul*, by Thomas More, a recreational distraction to clear her mind for more intellectual thoughts. Lucia rarely did anything by half measures, and the same held true here: her light reading commanded her full concentration. Still, her intense concentration was not enough to prevent a buzzing insect from drawing her attention. She swatted hard with her book at the insect, nearly hitting the young woman on the bench next to her.

"Aah!" the woman shrieked and ducked. "Professor! It's me! Beatriz!"

Stunned, Lucia apologized, "I'm so sorry, my dear! I didn't hit you, did I?" She dropped her book back into her bag. "My goodness, Beatriz. How long have you been sitting here?"

"Only forty-five minutes." Beatriz checked the time on her cell phone.

"Forty-five minutes! *Ayayay*! Where have I been?" Lucia chuckled. "And to mistake you for a mosquito or a bee, I must have been on some other planet." Lucia patted Beatriz's hand. "You know, *mi amiga*, patience is a virtue, but you could have interrupted me sooner!"

"But, Professor, you will be happy to know I have utilized every second of these forty-five minutes doing my homework, and I have made a great deal of progress."

"Then you are to be congratulated. But, Beatriz, certainly you don't feel the need to be in my presence to do your homework," Lucia chuckled. "So tell me, what brought you to find me?"

"I think the word for this is *kismet*," Beatriz noted. "I had to get out and take a walk. On the other side of the park, I came across Cathy. She told me she just left you sitting under this big tree by the kids playing ball."

The noisy soccer game continued. Lucia observed that more players joined since she last looked, a mass of young boys and girls frantically running and kicking the ball through goals defined by jackets and shoes. *What a pleasant afternoon,* she thought. "So now, Beatriz, what have you been patiently waiting to ask me?"

Her fists knotted tightly in her lap, Beatriz confessed, "Stress, Professor. This miserable stress is nearly killing me."

"What kind of stress? Grades? Taxes?" Lucia asked, immediately concerned. "Tell me the details. To help, I need specifics. Right now, you're talking in generalities."

Beatriz lowered her eyes, embarrassed to face her professor. "It's my boyfriend. He is very jealous. If he thinks I look at another man, he accuses me of cheating on him. He gets angry. He thinks if I'm watching TV and see a good-looking actor that I want to get on a plane to Hollywood. I swear, Professor, by my cross on this necklace my grandmother gave me that I am telling you the truth, and there is no way I would cheat on him."

Lucia sighed. She shook her head gently. "Shakespeare was right. Jealousy, the green-eyed monster," she mused. "Well, my friend, you cannot change another person. You can only change yourself. Let's see. Your boyfriend's attitude causes you to believe you are doing something terribly wrong, and so you stress yourself."

Beatriz's jaw dropped. "Me? I am stressing myself, Professor?" she asked incredulously. "I hate stress. I would never do that to myself."

"Pay attention," Lucia ordered. "Don't race ahead without all the facts, unless you want to stress yourself even more." Beatriz took a calming breath. Lucia added, "Did you know, Beatriz, that although stress may not be contagious, it is the most common illness that affects millions of people throughout the world?"

"Millions? Really?"

"No, you are right. I am wrong," Lucia admitted. "Billions." A giggle escaped Beatriz's lips. The mood lightened, and Lucia continued, "Do you know what stress is and what produces it?" Beatriz guessed, "Jealous boyfriends?"

"Hah!" Lucia said suddenly. "Yes, but not only jealous boyfriends. Typically, stress attacks many adults when they experience an accumulation of unfulfilled personal promises or when they face social and mechanical obstacles that interrupt the smooth flow of their choices—much like your boyfriend's jealousy—thus robbing them of the required emotional stability necessary for them to see themselves as happy people, like you right now.

"As I am sure you know, it seems no one has enough time to do all they feel they need to do anymore. Doesn't it seem that now time moves at the speed of lightning?" Lucia asked. Beatriz agreed, nodding vigorously.

"I think it was St Augustine who said 'speed does not increase time.' What the saint meant is while the minute always contains God's same old-fashioned sixty seconds, time can seem to move faster than those sixty seconds. And the more of our lives that we try to cram into those sixty seconds, the higher our stress level rises, leaving us with the feeling that we are not up to life's challenges."

Lucia's onslaught of information only served to confuse Beatrice, so she leaned close to whisper, "Tell me, Beatriz. Do you think that stress is a modern illness or has it existed throughout the ages?"

Calmed by the intimacy of whispers, Beatriz immediately answered, "My mother says stress is a new lifestyle because when she was little, her mother never talked of such a thing"

"Perhaps. But consider that all stress is not caused by the speed of life alone. What about lack of food? Or lack of work to earn money for shelter and food and to take care of your family?" Lucia became expansive, teaching one to one. "Beatriz, let me tell you that from my point of view, stress has always existed in one form or another as a human condition.

"Beatriz, do you remember the Stoics that we discussed in class?"

"Of course, Professor," Beatriz replied. "They were the Greek movement that began around the third century BC, weren't they?"

"Absolutely correct, my fine student," Lucia praised. "But do you remember their philosophy?"

Beatriz considered. "I think," she said hesitantly, "they believed if you made errors in judgment, that caused destructive emotions. But if you lived a pure, thoughtful life, you could strive to be a sage of moral and intellectual perfection and you would not suffer those emotions."

"You certainly remember the overview. Let's now look at some of the details: Those ancient Stoics created some very effective philosophical formulas that, when applied, can be very effective, like the best medicine, against the stress of our days.

"These ancient thinkers taught us about two kinds of powers. One power completely within our control is composed of temperance, emotional equilibrium, and equanimity of character. These are things we can always do something about. The other power consists of the things over which we have no control."

Beatriz brightened with the light of recognition. "The second one: that is the one that is killing me now. I have no control over the thoughts and feelings of my boyfriend."

Without warning, a scuffed soccer ball bounced into Lucia's lap. Both women jumped involuntarily. Then, Lucia held the ball in front of her. Three of the children, two boys and a girl, dashed toward them. Lucia notes, "This is a good example of what we are discussing. Neither you nor I had control over the motion of this ball surprising us."

Stopping several feet away, one of the boys called, "Please, lady, can we have our ball?"

"But now that we have the 'problem' in hand, we can control how we deal with it. The Stoics say we should not make an error in judgment or that will cause destructive emotions, right? So what are our choices?"

"The only one I can think of is to throw the ball back to them," Beatriz said.

"And, with that, you would be correct. That is the correct choice. But think about the other choices: we could keep the ball and take it home with us or we could simply ignore the children calling for their ball or we could take a sharp object and poke a hole in the ball and ruin it." Beatriz's eyes widened. Conspiratorially, Lucia asked, "You wouldn't have a pair of scissors or a knitting needle, would you?"

"Professor, you can't be serious," Beatriz gasped. "I would feel so guilty!"

"So the error in judgment causes destructive emotions then?" Lucia stood up.

"Then we will strive to be sages." She dropped the ball and expertly kicked it into the hands of the boy who called to them, impressing Beatriz.

"You see, the strength that is always up to us, according to the Stoics, is our *pride, courage*, and *dignity*. And the power that is never up to us is the opinion that other people maintain about us, in other words, our reputation." Lucia paced with determination, much as she did while teaching in the classroom. "Other things beyond our control include the inevitable loss of our dear ones, who leave us without asking us permission, without us being able to do anything to detain their eternal journey. And there are many more things beyond us, like the uncertain feeling of vulnerability. Have you ever been in the situation of never knowing if you have a job or not because we our employers can fire us or lay us off willy-nilly without a reason?"

"I, fortunately, have not been in that situation, but I know plenty of friends who have," Beatriz said.

"So, you can understand that regardless of your personal strength, control of your *reputation*, *family*, and *work* are beyond your abilities, and if you recognize it as such, you can avoid feelings of frustration and distress." Lucia searched her student's face for signs of understanding, then continued, "A lot of times when we do not know our human limits, we infect ourselves more gravely with self-imposed and unnecessary stress."

Beatriz concentrated hard, beginning to comprehend the concepts and apply them to her condition. "Then, how can I deal with the things that are not up to me without suffering all this stress?"

"Resign from it," Lucia said tersely.

"Resign?" Beatriz repeated, jaw dropping. "You mean, like, *quit*?"

Lucia softened. "In a way, yes. Remember in class, when we discussed personal philosophies? I believe you said your philosophy fell within the Judeo-Christian umbrella."

"I am a Christian," Beatriz asserted.

Lucia continued, "There is a Biblical term that can be very useful when unnecessary stress goes beyond remedy. That applicable word is 'resignation' because resignation is a kind of acceptance."

"Resignation is acceptance?" Beatriz echoed. "I'm not certain I get that."

Lucia resumed her seat next to Beatriz. Lucia took Beatriz's hand in hers.

"Do you remember, Beatriz, how difficult it was for you to accept the death of your grandmother?

"Yes," Beatriz said softly, remembering.

"I know well you miss her," Lucia said, equally softly. "Your grandmother was a good friend of mine too, and I miss her as well." Lucia gently lifted Beatriz's face. "Dear Beatriz, your emotions are much calmer now, are they not? Beatriz nodded. "You resigned yourself to accept your grandmother's departure. Since your *resignation*, you don't see it as a problem because there is no problem to solve because her death is now a *situation*. With that the case, stress does not play any role in that angle of your existence known as a *situation*. Because, in your words, you *quit* trying to solve a problem since it is a *situation* that cannot be solved."

"I think I am beginning to understand, Professor," Beatriz brightened. "When something is completely beyond my control to change, if I accept that and resign myself to understand it is beyond my individual power, then it will stop being a problem and resolve into a *situation*."

"That is the essence." Lucia smiled.

"So," said Beatriz, her mood darkening, "I must resign myself to stop stressing over my *reputation* as my boyfriend sees it and accept he believes I am cheating even though it is a lie?"

Self-involved with her own ideas, Lucia answered, "If you apply the advice of these ancient Greek thinkers, you learn to dominate the unnecessary stress before it becomes a mental burden and prevent the stress from becoming physiological. Deal with the problem now before it manifests itself in your personality, causing you to feel tormented as if stress were a chronic illness that could almost be inherited."

"That doesn't really answer my question," Beatriz said, pouting a bit. "You're saying I just have to live with my boyfriend's jealousy?" Surprised by the question, Lucia returned from her reverie to the immediate. Lucia thought a moment and held out her hand. "Come. Walk with me."

They walked north, the bright sun to their left. To their right, the soccer game wound down. Moms and Dads called to their children, who gathered shoes, jackets, and ball and ran to them. The flamboyantly dressed skater zipped by, mimicking a horn, "beep, beep" as he passed.

Lucia took Beatriz's arm as they proceeded. "You came to me with a very specific question. Now I will give you a very specific answer. We have to learn to become genuine and authentic. For example, when a question is asked, it is important to answer with a genuine 'yes' or 'no' and stop the tendency to be ambivalent. I am afraid I have danced around your question with my explanation of Stoic philosophy but understand I had my reasons. As the playwright Edward Albee once wrote, 'Sometimes it is necessary to go a long way out of your way in order to come back a short distance correctly.' Do you follow me, Beatriz?"

"I am trying, Professor," Beatriz said weakly.

"Let me illustrate 'yes or no' versus 'ambivalence.' Someone asks me for a favor, say, 'Will you take this unmarked brown paper bag to a dark corner in the barrio and give it to a man with an eye patch and gang tattoos.' Now, that is a favor that I'd rather not fulfill, but out of fear, I give an ambivalent answer and say, 'Sure, I'll be glad to help you,' and after that, I regret my answer. I then realize that I put myself in jeopardy because, when the favor was presented to me as a question, that was the precise moment to be genuine and honest with my answer and say a definitive no!"

Understanding crept into Beatriz's eyes. Lucia continued, "Here's another example: I know of a woman, who after twenty-three years of marriage, sick and tired of always being the one to take the dirty shirts to the cleaners, one day said to her husband, "Dear, do you think you could pick up your clean shirts from the cleaners?"

"Of course," answered the husband. "As a matter of fact, why don't I take the dirty ones since I am going to collect the clean ones. I might as well do that from now on. I always drive by the cleaners anyway." The woman could hardly believe that from one second to the next she was no longer responsible for the burden she had carried for twenty-three years because she had finally asked a very direct and sincere question to her husband. What a difference!"

"The women created her own burden ever since the first dirty shirt. Hadn't she, Professor?"

"Yes, Beatriz, because for twenty-three years, she lacked the strength of character to be honest with her husband. I believe I see you have understood very well my explanation."

"Oh my goodness!" Beatriz laughed. "Why do we believe we are capable of knowing what the other person thinks as if we have ESP that tells us what the other person wants to understand?"

"You are correct, my fine student," Lucia said. She stopped near another bench, close to the northwest corner of the park. "Before we part," Lucia added seriously," let's sit down for a minute because I have something important to ask you." They settled on the bench beside the walk. "Now, Beatriz, you came to me for help to deal with your jealous boyfriend. I told you of the Stoics philosophies, which led to discussing the dangers of ambivalence. But, what you ask me cannot be treated lightly because your decision will affect the course of your life, which makes me very concerned for you."

The depth and gravity of Lucia's challenge and concern came to Beatriz. Lucia observed the rapid changes on Beatriz's face caused by her consideration of multiple options and outcomes.

"I am not asking you to give me your definitive yes or no now," Lucia assured softly. "If you make a choice you subsequently feel is wrong, you have the power to make a new choice to correct your errant decision. You must remember you have plenty of personal pride, courage, and dignity to take care of yourself. As you stated so well, you don't have ESP to know what the other person thinks, or as I have mentioned to you in class, my eleventh commandment: 'Thou shall not think for the other.' And if you constantly try to bend to what you believe the other person wants, you make yourself subject to one of our biggest causes of unnecessary stress."

Tears formed in Beatriz's eyes. "Thank you, Professor, for your care and advice," she said.

Lucia dug into her bag. "But, let's not confuse questions with commands. Let's learn to apply the best of us, and let's experiment each day to find ways stress can be a thing of the past." Lucia found her packet of tissues and offered it. Beatriz wiped her tears and managed a bit of a smile. Abruptly, Lucia stood up. "Let's learn to enjoy those tranquil and authentic godlike sixty seconds as St Augustine would have liked us to do. Come, let's walk to the corner."

Beatriz remained on the park bench. "Professor, I think I will enjoy the precious sixty seconds of every minute right here while I ponder my decision."

"Very well," Lucia said. "I know you will make a good one."

"Professor?" Beatriz added with quick urgency, "I am going to say 'no' to my boyfriend. I mean I am going to say 'no' to our relationship. I mean, I realize the positive change has to come from me, and the only way to do that is to make him move out."

"That's a possible outcome."

"It is more than possible," Beatriz asserted, "because my name is on the lease and his isn't."

"And you are certain about this?" Lucia queried.

"Certain, with no ambivalence. I confess I am concerned about confronting James, but I can already feel my decision lifting the stress from my mind. I must thank you again, Professor," Beatriz said.

"None of this is easy," Lucia advised. "Would you like for me to stay with you here on the bench while you think?"

"I'm fine, and I think I need to sit here by myself with my thoughts. But thanks for your offer and your caring for me. I will be fine, using the Stoics philosophy."

"Then I will see you soon. And feel free to seek my help and advice whenever you like. And I say that with *no* ambivalence," Lucia said, gathering her bag.

Lucia strode away, glancing back once to see Beatriz, alone on the bench, in peaceful repose with her thoughts. With a firm and steady gait, Lucia reached the corner as the traffic light changed and allowed her to cross the avenue without stopping, and she headed to her home, embracing that internal joy of satisfaction she felt every time she helped someone.

Sublime Eternal Truth or Poisonous Lies

U PON HER ARRIVAL, Lucia's loyal husband Gary greeted her
with a tall glass of lemonade. In the kitchen, her daughters,
Laura and Ellen, prepared dinner and set the table for the family's
evening meal.

Lucia loved teaching so much that she even taught night classes.
But, when she didn't, she enjoyed dining with her whole family just
the way she did when she was young. This custom she did not want to
lose.

In the midst of the meal, Laura said, "By the way, Mom, I wonder if
you recall Mrs. Johnson's niece Caroline?"

"Of course, I do," responded Lucia. "Why?"

"Caroline is coming to see you at eight. She is desperate to talk with
you."

"Did she tell you why she needs to talk with me?" Lucia asked,
furrowing her brow.

"No, she didn't say, but she seemed quite upset."

"Then we'll soon see, won't we?" Lucia said as she rose from the
table.

Lucia fetched a little pitcher full of water and went from room
to room watering her violets. She allowed no one else to do this job,
insisting that watering violets is not a simple task. Extreme care needs
to be taken so that water does not touch the leaves as it could burn them.
More to the point, Lucia found the act of watering quite therapeutic.

At eight o'clock on the button, Caroline arrived. "Lucia, I am so
glad to be able to come and talk with you," she said anxiously.

"Come in, *mija*," Lucia said soothingly, using the Spanish term of
endearment for a daughter, her arm around Caroline's shoulders. "Tell

me, what is going on? You appear quite nervous or upset. I can't tell which one."

"It is both, my dear Professor, *both*! I am, as they say, between a rock and a hard place."

"Please come and sit down." It was clear that Caroline was extremely upset. Lucia called to her son Sam to bring coffee. Lucia smiled warmly at Caroline and patted her hand. Caroline smiled tightly. "Now then, if I may," Lucia said, "allow me to share with you the wisdom of the great Greek philosopher, Aristotle. This wise man talked about three concepts: nutrition, perception, and reason. Aristotle observed that plants need *nutrition*, animals need *perception*, and human beings need *reason* because, as Aristotle would say, 'man is a social animal by nature.' So, when we make a choice, we must recognize that, before the physical choice is made (the action), the mental choice is already conceived. Therefore, we are already able to anticipate the outcome: pleasure or pain, success or failure."

Caroline blushed and looked down at her hands in her lap. She realized she had not been prudent with her most recent choice and created her own problem. Lucia paused. She observed Caroline reddening. "I'm sorry. You came to me with a problem to solve, and here I am expounding about Aristotle. Tell me, what brings you to see me?"

"Do you remember my childhood friend Andrea?"

"Of course! I remember her very well. The two of you were always together."

Sam arrived with coffee. The two women sipped. Lucia breathed a loud "Aaaaaaah!" which made Caroline smile. The hot drink warmed their moods. Lucia continued, "About Andrea, is she okay?" Caroline gave a weak smile. "Yes, she's fine, but *I* am not. She called me the other day to tell me that she had a few free days and that she wanted to spend them with me. The more excited she got about visiting me, the more *I* tried to get *rid* of her. It's not that I don't love her, but now is just not the right time to visit me." Caroline sagged into the sofa, miserable with her dilemma.

"So far I don't see any problem with you telling her that," said Lucia.

"If only I had told her just that," said Caroline. "Instead, I lied and told her that I had a trip coming up. I said that my boss was sending me to Washington, DC, on the very day she wanted to come see me. She said that she understood my situation, and we hung up. At that second, I chuckled and congratulated myself on how easily I got rid of Andrea."

"Oh my, now you have to live your own lie," said Lucia.

"But, that's not all," Caroline said. "A few hours later, Andrea called again, but I didn't answer. She left a message telling me that she had so many free flying miles she had decided to buy a ticket to DC! Her plan was that while I was working, she would visit the Smithsonian museum and the White House. By evening we could have dinner together and have a nice visit. She was so happy, and I have made such a mess!"

Lucia's mind drifted to one of her favorite lectures. "Caroline," she said, "it is for this reason Plato tells us that *we must think before we act*. Aristotle would match that advice with the following: (1) When one has to make a decision, the choice must be made keeping two things in mind: the *nobility* of our ethical commitment, that it always be guided by *reason*. (2) One must learn to calculate using one's animal perception toward the benefit that that choice will *actually* bring. (3) If everything is well balanced, then one can count on physical pleasure, just like plants benefit from the earth's nutrients. Does this make sense to you, Caroline?"

Caroline was baffled. "I am sorry, Professor, but I don't understand what any of that has to do with me or my problem."

Lucia took Caroline's hand and spoke gently. "What happened to you is that you forgot to think of the benefit that comes from speaking the *truth*. This *truth* is what builds your *noble* character. But you skipped all of that to pursue only the pleasure of your choice when you tried to get rid of your friend. This is why you find yourself between a rock and a hard place and are experiencing anxiety, embarrassment, and guilt. What you have, Caroline, is an *ethical disaster*, and now you have neither *pleasure*, *benefit*, nor *nobility*. We must always remember that the *truth* is something *sublime* and *eternal* while lies are corrupting and poisonous."

"What am I going to do when Andrea finds out that I lied to her?" said Caroline, nearly in tears.

"Now I am going to speak to you the way therapists do some times and that is with *detached caring*. It is hard to know how Andrea is likely to respond, but when you speak the truth, while you may be risking your friendship, you may also be regaining self-respect, plus releasing the burden and pressure caused by guilt. It's always good to remember that *guilt* presents itself when *one could have acted otherwise*. And yes, I may sound to you somewhat *detached* from your pain but keep in mind that I do it *caring*."

"Ah, Professor, you are quite right," Caroline said with embarrassment. "Now I must go and pay the consequence of my unethical choice."

"And that, my dear, takes courage, but I know as my friend Jane likes to say it, *'You can do it*,'" said Lucia, smiling while closing the door behind Caroline.

"Didn't she like the coffee?" Sam asked, leaning around the door.

To Err Is Human. Or Is It?

ACH THIRD SATURDAY of the month at Kat's Café, Lucia presided over a Socratic social group. Her old friend Kat appreciated the favor; it brought her a regular group of customers for her coffee, cakes, hors d'oeuvres, and sandwiches on a Saturday evening when folks went to trendier places to dine. It took little effort for Kat. She brought in a chalkboard and some extra chairs. She didn't mind that Beatriz often brought in a tray of home-baked cookies—that increased sales of coffee and soft drinks.

Lucia structured the evening around the Socratic method, using the dialectic approach of question and answer. Lucia always looked forward to the third Saturday of each month. After so many years in the classroom, conducting these sessions was second nature.

Her participants streamed in between seven thirty and eight, ordered their cups of coffee and selected noshes, took their seats, and readied for Lucia's lecture.

"Good evening, my dear colleagues," she began. Lucia liked to use the term "colleagues" because she felt a sense of philosophical connection. For Lucia, it was very important to make sure that all of those present were ready to share one very specific thing in common. Lucia always asked first if everyone was willing to share their "intellectual ignorance." It was a successful icebreaker, helping every one relax and eager to engage.

"I am very glad to be with you, my dear friends, on this beautiful Saturday evening. For this occasion, I want to talk to you about the world of philosophical contrast, and I hope we become successful in understanding this theme. But please do not forget, regardless of how aggressive I may get while speaking, please interrupt me and ask any questions."

The assembled group nodded and mumbled assents.

"Our philosophical theme tonight is to understand the difference between *truth and falsity, correct and incorrect, good and evil, just and unjust, beauty and ugliness, etc.* This seems to be our eternal dilemma because no one likes to be wrong, but we all continue to make mistakes. First, I want to tell you that according to Plato—the greatest Greek philosopher—for him, human errors are completely unnecessary."

"But no one is perfect," a blustery bald man sitting in the back of the group said in a loud voice.

"Let me tell you that for now, you are correct, but allow me to continue. As we all know we have the ability to think, but we need to go beyond just thinking. Buddha spoke of us having six senses and not five. The sixth sense for Buddha is the ability to 'think thinking' or as Plato might state, 'we must think reasoning.'"

The man snorted. "Excuse me, Lucia, but isn't to think the same thing as to reason?"

"That is a wonderful observation," Lucia noted. "But look, we spend all day thinking the same way we spend all day breathing. However, the moment we need to make a choice—as small as it may be—at that very moment, we stop just thinking, and we start reasoning. Do you see what I mean?"

"Okay, okay. I get it," the man said, frowning and nodding.

Lucia picked up the chalk. "Look," she said, "I am going to draw a circle." Extending her arm, she made an arcing sweep as if she were a big compass going all the way around 360 degrees.

A murmur rose from the group. "Oh my god, your circle is perfect!" and "What a great job!" they said.

"Thank you very much for your nice comments," said Lucia, smiling at the flattery. "But, now I want you to truly judge my circle, and I'll assure you that you will see that it is not perfect."

"Well," said Beatriz, "it's almost perfect."

"Thank you, Beatriz. But note you used the descriptor *almost perfect.* You see, we know that my circle is not perfect." Drawing the others into her reasoning, Lucia said, "It is obvious as you take a good look, you can tell that my circle is a circle—not a square or a triangle. But, the moment we decide to evaluate its perfection as a circle, it is that precise moment that we move from perceiving to reasoning, and we begin to use our intelligence instead of our emotions in order to avoid any fanciful theory of 'perfection.' Haven't we heard Alexander Pope's famous saying 'To err is human'?"

Beatriz said, "That's because nobody's perfect."

"True, Beatriz. Very true. But while we know that is a fact, should we use it as an excuse to continue making mistakes so long as we insist that 'nobody is perfect'?"

The assembled group murmured in quiet discussion among themselves. Noting this, Lucia said, "It seems to me that this is a good time to take a little break, get a refill of coffee, and enjoy one more of those delicious cookies that Beatriz made for us as the model of the 'perfect' cookies or Kat's 'perfect' cakes."

Some of the group chose to stay in their chairs; others got up and went straight to the blackboard to attempt the drawing of the perfect circle. Others headed to the counter for more coffee. A short line formed at the women's restroom, and two or three dashed out to the sidewalk for a cigarette break.

After a few minutes, Lucia continued. "Let me tell you that in Plato's most valuable book, *The Republic*, there is a very famous quote that says more or less the following, 'Unless the philosopher becomes a king and the king becomes a philosopher, there will be no justice in the world.'"

A young woman, Sarah, raised her hand. "Lucia, could you repeat that one more time?" Most of the others wanted that, too.

"Absolutely. I will gladly repeat that celebrated phrase." This time, Lucia. standing up as a priest may do in his church, repeated, "Unless the philosopher becomes a king and the king becomes a philosopher, there will be no justice in the world." She emphasized, "Now let me tell you that this is a *paradox* because the fact is, the majority of us are neither philosophers nor kings."

Lucia barely finished her thought when Sarah asked, "But what is paradox?"

"Of course," said Lucia. "According to the dictionary, the term 'paradox' comes from the Greek words *para* and *doxa*, and this means beyond the incredible. In simple terms, it is like when we say someone wants to have their cake and eat it too. One makes the other impossible. But metaphorically speaking, according to Plato, we actually can have our cake and eat it. Think for a second what part of you could be the philosopher and what part of you could be the king. Generally the philosopher advises and the king executes because the philosopher represents the ideas and the king represents the actions. It is good to know that Plato's philosophy carries the idea that makes him the *idealist*, and Aristotle's philosophy carries the actions that make him the *empiricist*."

With little to do at the counter, Kat had drifted to the back row of chairs. "Lucia, could you give us an example?" she asked.

"That is a good idea. Imagine ideas and actions moving in a parallel line like the tracks of the railroad. Intellectually, we know these tracks go to their destination still in parallel beyond the horizon. Yet when we look at the tracks toward the horizon, they appear to meet, contradicting what we know as a fact. And this is a paradox.

"But let me give another example, changing the idea. Let me ask you a question. Has anyone of you experienced the feeling of success?"

"I have!" Beatriz exclaimed as she recalled getting an A+ in her physics exam and also feeling a bit embarrassed as she demonstrated her enthusiasm in front of everyone.

"Thank you, Beatriz. That feeling of success you feel is due to the perfect association of *cause and effect*. If we become aware and vigilant about the continuity of *cause and effect relationships*, this will help us to count the series of perfect moments that we experience all day long, and thus we may learn to appreciate the presence of happiness as a tangible reality, the same way that we feel the sense of success. I will never forget that when my youngest daughter, Alexandria, would arrive at home a few minutes before I did, she would go inside the house using the side gate. In order to make sure that she was not going to get hurt by stepping on or tripping over my husband's tools in that route, I taught her to walk the 'easy road,' watching her little feet and saying at the same time 'cause-effect, cause-effect,' and every time when she arrived, she would be very proud of herself and tell me that she had done her 'cause-effect' walking. As we all know, the feeling of success is due to the accumulative momentum of *good habits* because *good habits* guarantee good results. For example, *cause* may equal 'if I follow a good diet.' *However, the thought* 'if I follow a good diet' is an empty thought until I am able to say, 'Effect equals I am on a healthy diet, and therefore I am feeling healthy.'

"On the other hand, we become victims of our incomplete thought if we stop at 'if I quit smoking,' 'if I pay my bills,' 'if I didn't use my credit card for unnecessary things,' 'if I didn't drink so much,' etc. *Nature forgets nothing!* That is to say, if we do not complete the thought with appropriate action, we will not achieve the effect we want. Think for a moment of all those wonderful Olympic winners whose daily good habits give them the opportunity to win."

"What about the people who believe that they always have bad luck?" asked the bald man in the back row.

"Consider this," Lucia said, directing her comment to the man. "People who have what we call *good* luck are usually people with healthy, productive, and positive ideas, who know how to make a reality of those positive thoughts. Somehow these *lucky* people have either a learned or innate ability to think scientifically in order to avoid disasters."

"Lucia," said Judy, a girl with long hair and narrow frame glasses, "I know the scientific method. Is that the same as the scientific way of thinking?"

"In a way. Both involve consequential thinking, like those who put in practice the *philosophy* then the *execution*, like the king does."

"I'm not . . . Can you clarify that?" asked Kat.

"Imagine that someone asks you to meet at 3:00 AM in Drug Sale Barrio. That very second you would say, 'Are you out of your mind?' Did you see how fast you came up with an answer? That shows you how quickly the brain can work. Your mental reaction is the *philosopher*, and your answer, 'Are you out of your mind?' is the response executed by the *king* in you.

"Thus, when we have the time to think through our commitments, we must take the advantage of that time to move philosophically from thinking to reasoning. My advice to you is stay away from unnecessary commitments when someone surprises you. Say that a person asks you a favor. You think you need to say *yes* because, out of politeness, you don't want to say *no*. Why not say, 'Let me think about it for a few minutes.' After all, that person is the one who needs you! And a lot of times, the most magic word for those reluctant favors is just '*no!*' That says it all.

"My suggestion for all of you is keep learning, keep studying, or finish your college degree. While you are in college, you will experience hundreds of tests, exams, multiple choices, presentations, etc. Every one of those exams will be preparing you to become '*a problem-solving personality*' and will teach you also to develop *critical thinking skills* that move you from perceiving to reasoning."

"What about imagination?" Again the man in back challenged Lucia. "What role does imagination play between perceiving and reasoning?"

"Are you wondering about Einstein?" Lucia asked him. The entire group turned to look at the man, now impressed that he may have caught Lucia in a conundrum.

"Yes," he stated, confidently.

"Then you may know that Einstein said, 'Imagination is more important than knowledge.' Which can be true, I suppose. A lot of people know a lot, but if they allow themselves to spend all their time imagining, they *think* they know it all and are the worst for it." The man in the back scowled.

"Can I ask how what we've been talking about could apply to this girl I know who got into a heck of a mess with this guy?" asked Judy.

Lucia checked her watch. "We have only a few minutes left. Let's put it to the group. Do you want to hear about this girl Judy knows, or do you want me to finish my lecture?" To a person, they wanted to hear about the girl. Lucia nodded to Judy. "Go ahead."

"Well," said Judy, "one day my friend Hope met this guy. Hope's not my BFF or anything. Sometimes we just hang out between classes. Hope said this guy was handsome, charming, and wonderful, and she, like, fell in love at first sight. You know, like she had wedding bells going off in her brain. And with that idea fixed in her head, all she had to do was make sure that this guy Frank fell in love with her. Hope figured that if she didn't ask too many questions and just allowed Frank to share with her whatever he wanted, he'd fall in love with her like she did with him. And that's how it seemed to work.

"So, like, six months went by. Hope took him to meet everybody in her family. He never took her to meet any of his family or his friends. She wanted to ask him real badly about that, but she had pressured other boys in the past, and they dropped her like a hot rock. And one day without warning, Frank disappeared."

"What do you mean, he disappeared?" Lucia asked.

"You know, like *gone*. Like vanished off the face of the Earth. Like *kaputski*. But like, a long time before, once when he left his cell phone on the bar when he went to the little boy's room, Hope got his home phone number. She never called it because he always used his cell, but she had his number. So she calls. And this woman answers. And Hope says she wants to speak to Frank. And the woman says, 'This is Barbara. Can I help you?' And Hope says, no, she wants to talk to Frank. And the woman kind of sighs like this has happened before and says to Hope that she and Frank are married and all, and she hopes that Hope didn't let him get all up in her stuff because Frank's not going nowhere, not with Willy counting on him. And then the woman says to Hope that she used to be just like Hope except it was with Hilary. And Hope says, 'Who is Hilary?' And the woman says Hilary is Frank's first ex-wife, and she, Barbara may be his second ex-wife, and that Hope doesn't want to be his third ex-wife. And by the way, Willy is his eight-year-old son, and he has a six-month-old baby daughter. And the woman said, 'I hope to God you're not calling to tell him he has another baby mamma.' And she hung up.

"As you can imagine," Judy recounted, "by now Hope felt completely devastated. And now I realize as you were trying to explain that if Hope had used her *reasoning*, she could have saved all that unnecessary pain."

"You are absolutely correct," said Lucia. "Poor Hope suffered because she allowed herself to be taken by her *imagination* and the *world of appearances*. Hope limited herself to only *belief* instead of pursuing *knowledge*. She didn't know that Frank was a liar, and if she had insisted on knowing some of the facts of his life, he would have disappeared a lot sooner. This is why Plato's greatest advice is *'Think before you act'*."

Conversation among the group rose to a clamor with everyone coming up with alternatives that Hope could have taken and methods to punish Frank. Lucia interrupted, telling them that Judy's story was a good example and not an opportunity to redeem Hope or execute Frank.

"The main philosophical point to apply right now is Plato's own words: *'Unless the philosophers becomes kings or the kings or rulers come to be sufficiently inspired with a genuine desire for wisdom there can be no rest from troubles because it is hard to see that there is no other way of happiness for the state or the individual.'* And now this seems to me a good ending for our philosophical chat. As I anticipate the privilege to be with you within three weeks."

The meeting broke up happily. Even the guy in the back helped put the café back in order. Kat efficiently stored the food and almost all said their good-byes, except Judy, who had more to tell Lucia about Hope.

Lucia listened patiently. *Ayayay!*

9

Freedom and Liberty

A LOUD AND urgent pounding came from Lucia's front door, rousing her from her home office where she worked on her latest book. "Coming, coming, coming!" she called, hurrying to the door.

A quick look out the window alongside the doorframe told her the knocker was her friend Adele from across the street, looking upset. Lucia opened the door and asked, "Are you okay? What's wrong?"

"Oh, Lucia," Adele said, holding back tears. "The police just came to my house!"

"The police? Come in. Let me get you some tea." Lucia guided Adele back to the kitchen. "Is Eduardo all right? And Ann?" Lucia had dread thoughts about Adele's husband and college-age daughter.

"No, it's my nephew Alfonso. I *lied*, Lucia! I can't believe I lied to the police." Adele collapsed to a chair and covered her face, sobbing loudly. Lucia embraced her.

"I started water for Chamomile tea. It will calm your nerves. Now, what sort of lie did you tell the police and why did they come to your house?"

Adele wiped her tears. "They wanted to know if Alfonso was with me two nights ago. I said he was, but it was a lie, Lucia. I haven't seen him for nearly two months. I guessed he told them he was with me, otherwise why would they have come to my house?"

Lucia sat down at the table, waiting for the kettle to boil. "You know how we talk about the shows on TV where they figure out mysteries from clues? Let's try that. You asked the question. What can you figure out?"

"I saw a story on the eleven o'clock news that a gang robbed the bodega at Fourteenth and Elm two nights ago. They said they thought it was connected to a couple other robberies."

"And you think Alfonso is involved?"

"Estella has been so worried that he's taking up with a gang. When he was younger, he always did so well in school. Now, he's failing everything. He shaved his head, his pants hang down so his underwear shows. I have trouble even thinking about it." More tears flowed.

The kettle whistled merrily, and Lucia prepared two cups. "Call your sister. Find out where Alfonso is now and if she wants us to help out," Lucia instructed.

From Estella, Adele learned that Alfonso was supposed to be in school—*supposed* being the active word. And Estella did want their help. She was also worried what her husband would do if he found out Alfonso was hanging with a gang and robbing merchants.

"What school does he go to?" Lucia asked.

"Martin Luther King Junior Middle," Adele replied.

"How old is he?" Lucia asked, surprised.

"He just turned thirteen."

"A very difficult age. Lots of hormones. Trying to figure out his place in the world. Hopefully, we caught him in time."

Lucia and Adele sat in Adele's car in front of the school, waiting for classes to end. The facade needed renovation, and certainly the inside needed work, but the city and state governments cut budgets, and there was no money. "How can we expect young people to do well if we don't show them respect by providing a positive place of learning?" Lucia wondered.

The final bell rang and students spilled out of the building. "There he is," Adele noted, pointing out a short, skinny kid mingling with other boys dressed like him.

"Call him over," Lucia said.

"What you doing, yo Auntie?" the young man asked, swaggering up.

"We thought you could use a ride home." Adele said brightly.

Alfonso nervously eyed Lucia. He glanced back over his shoulder. "I'm-a hanging with my homies, yo. How come you ridin' with the professor?" He studiously avoided eye contact with Lucia.

"We're going to the Ocho," Lucia told him. "Hop in. I'll treat you to a milk shake. A big one. You look like you could use the calories."

Alfonso considered. The Ocho, a well-established sweetshop known for its ice cream treats had been a magnet for generations of teens. It had become less fashionable as of late, and prices had risen steeply. The temptation got the better of him, and Alfonso ducked into the backseat.

Slipping down below window level, Alfonso demanded, "Drive, Auntie, drive. I don't want my homeboys to see me."

Adele pulled away. Lucia turned around and said, "I know what you mean. Your auntie and I have to be concerned with our reputations too." Alfonso sulked, feeling like he had just been dissed.

Pulling up in front of the Ocho, Lucia told Adele to expect her call when they were ready to be picked up. She wanted to talk with Alfonso alone.

Alfonso preceded her into the shop to be met by Mr. Washington behind the counter saying, "No! You can't come in here! Turn around and go back out." Washington had a sign with a long list of no's: no saggers, no colors, no gang signs . . . and many others. Lucia insisted that Alfonso was with her for ice cream and nothing else. Mr. Washington relented. He needed the business.

They took a table in the corner. Alfonso insisted on sitting with his back to the wall. He sipped hard on his straw, his eyes darting around the room suspiciously.

"How's the shake?" Lucia asked.

"Good," Alfonso replied, still not looking at her.

Lucia began, "You know, Alfonso, I am a philosopher."

Startled, he asked, "Parole officer?" taken by surprise.

"No, philosopher. I use my thinking skills to analyze ways to live. There have been many of us through the history of man. You and I can talk about ways to live, can we not, Alfonso?"

"You mean you talk, and I pretend to listen, like in Mr. Hopper's Algebra 1."

"How about I talk, and you tell me what you hear?"

"Sure," Alfonso sneered. "You talk, and I call BS."

"Let's see, then. 'I'm going to do anything I want, and I don't care what anyone says.' Agree, Alfonso?" Lucia looked at him for an answer.

"Yeah. That's what my homie Combo says."

"All right. Tell me how this Combo does whatever he wants and doesn't care. Give me an example."

Alfonso thought, sipping pensively. "Okay. Okay. I got it. Combo never got his learner's and never got his license, but like, he's sixteen, you know, so he uses his mother's car and drives. And he gets stopped by the Five-O, and they give him a ticket and impound his mom's car, and she goes all crazy and stuff, but Combo has, like, this stash of cash and him and his mom go down to the lot and get her car, and he's back behind the wheel in, like, two hours."

"And what did he have to say for himself?"

"Yeah, he said having a piece of paper didn't have nothing to do with driving. Combo said the cops are stupid because he knows how to drive, and they can't stop him."

"Well, Alfonso, he was neither thinking nor reasoning. He was simply rationalizing."

"I don't know what that means," Alfonso answered sullenly.

"The difference is that in reasoning, we use the capacity to think and calculate, but when we rationalize, we use what we think are legitimate excuses for our defense. So, in light of that, Combo needs to rationalize his behavior, or he'll have to admit that if he drives without a license, he is abusing his freedom and his liberty."

Alfonso snorted rudely. Lucia took a calming breath and continued. "Liberty gives *legal* permission. The driver's license gives legal permission to drive, a hunting license gives legal permission to hunt, and when one qualifies for a driving or hunting license, it means that one is a good citizen."

Lucia sensed the young man's attention drifting, but she was not about to slow down. She slapped the table top, and his instinctive reaction brought him back.

"Okay, here's the deal: if you're looking for the definition of freedom and the definition of liberty, they both appear to have similar meanings. Freedom is the state of not being imprisoned, enslaved, or otherwise constrained. Liberty is the right and power to act, believe, or express oneself in a manner of one's own choosing. I am telling you that there is more to this. Liberty is society's way of giving you permission to do the things you love, like driving. You're given license to do this. Freedom, on the other hand, embodies your own *personal* liberty. You have an *existential personal choice* to think freely, choose freely, decide, love, hate freely, and so on. No one can take this kind of freedom away from you. I hope I've made this clear for you. You are . . . ah . . . *free* to say no, of course!"

Several words caught Alfonso's attention: freedom, imprisoned, permission, liberty, personal choice. Still, her avalanche of words confused him. "But Combo said that he's gonna drive till he gets caught again."

With a sigh, Lucia responded, "Dear Alfonso, that attitude is *precisely* the one that goes against divine wisdom and freedom." Lucia realized all this was a bit much for her young friend. She said gently, "Let's step back and start with a new beginning. Let's start with this premise—idea—laws are made to be obeyed. This is what keeps societies in order. If we didn't have laws, everything would be in chaos. The ancient philosopher Socrates wrote about exactly this."

"Who?"

"Socrates. He was . . . I'll tell you more about him another time if you're interested. Let's stay on track. First, do you know you are following this as well as my college students?"

"I am?"

"You are." Alfonso brightened. He sat up and no longer glanced about the room. This lady philosopher said he was smart, and nobody besides his mother said that very much.

Lucia observed the change in his physicality. She said, "I have a sneaking suspicion that once you learn a few basic ideas and concepts you will have a *paradigm shift* that will amaze you. Bear with me as I give you a quick lesson about a few very important concepts: law, prohibition, maturity, wisdom, conscience, human wisdom, and reason, to name a few. And along the way, you will learn about an amazing three-part construct in your soul that rules your life."

"Souls are for church," Alfonso noted.

"You only have a soul when you're in church? I think your soul is you all the time. Do you want another milk shake?" Lucia asked. He shook his head. "Okay, I am going to say something that you won't like. Just listen, and we'll talk because I want to hear your ideas, Saint Thomas Aquinas, from the eleventh century, said this about the law, *'a law is a command'* or an *order* that must to be followed. Laws are written to be obeyed and bring about social order. When a law is not obeyed, it is because those who lack maturity do not like anything that is an order or forbids them to do a certain thing. They feel that it prohibits them from satisfying their wants and needs. Maturity comes when it is understood *why* a law is to be obeyed."

Alfonso sighed loudly. Lucia ignored that. "We must stop at a stop sign or a red light, is this not correct, Alfonso? You may get angry, curse and complain all you want about your forward progress being interrupted, but if someone runs lights and stop signs, there are going to be lots of accidents."

"I get it." Alfonso answered dourly.

"But," the professor continued, "when we feel anger and we think that we have no choice but to obey the law, this is when a law becomes a prohibition rather than an obligation. Nobody likes to be told they can't do something they feel like they want to do." Alfonso stopped sulking and focused his attention. Lucia said, "A perfect example is the child who obeys his parents out of fear of the potential spanking. When fear becomes the only motive for obedience, the child is no longer truly responsible for his behavior. She is not mature enough yet to reason. But remember, lack of maturity can be found at any age."

Alfonso blinked at the professor, taking in this fact and applying it to himself. It was dawning on Alfonso that the lady philosopher just might be on to something. "So, to continue this analogy, when a child is willful, and she chooses to do whatever she pleases, she justifies her behavior, saying, 'I do what I want when I want, like your homeboy Combo."

With this reasoning brought full circle, Alfonso grasped the ideas and felt self-satisfaction. He didn't show it though. He did not want to reward Lucia for that.

"Do you remember how I said that there is a three-part construct within yourself that rules your life? Well, our Socrates believed that within us, in our soul, we have the three forms of government. I'm certain you have learned about the three 'branches' of government in school, right? What are they?"

"Legislative, executive, and judicial," Alfonso stated flatly, surprised he remembered from seventh-grade civics.

"That's right," said Lucia. "Socrates talked about a whole Supreme Court in our soul. St. Thomas Aquinas called it the voice of one's conscience, whose engine is the capacity to reason, the reason that is illuminated by wisdom. And when we go against our own capacity to reason, we are actually disobeying human laws and divine laws."

Alfonso furrowed his brow. *This is really complicated,* he thought, and yet he felt it was really interesting at the same time.

"Okay then, Alfonso, I'm going to just add a little more. When two people break the law, each is using individual freedom. This is the reason that *there is no collective sin.* It is very important not to blame, regardless of what happened. When the difference between freedom and liberty is understood and put in practice accordingly, that is when one becomes mature. But if blame is put into practice, the meaning of

MARÍA ELENA PELLINEN

acting in good will is not to be known. And that, my dear boy, is another lecture!

"Let's take one more look at freedom. It is a gift, certainly, and the way Aristotle explains it, when put into practice, is a noble choice. Aristotle was Plato's student for twenty years," she said, dropping in this bit to hold his interest. "Then, as I was saying, when one puts into practice freedom, attached to good will, one may then enjoy *spiritual tranquility*.

"If this is not put into practice, we become blinded to the gift of freedom. We choose to fall into error and allow ourselves to be dragged by temptation. Before we know, we have left the *capacity to reason* behind. The temptation to break the law becomes the most absurd choice of conduct. Furthermore, eventually the transcendental consequences of this behavior such as stress, anxiety, dread, panic, and loneliness envelop us. We, as humans, feel the need to talk about choices we've made, but it is never easy to tell anyone about our wrong choices. Unfortunately, we may confide in someone with an even more corrupted soul. They may seem to give us a lift, assuring us that the things we've done were nothing compared to what they have done. It's easy to get a false sense of security.

"You mean, like, Combo?"

"If you want to take that from our talk, I won't stop you. So, Alfonso, be very careful with this attitude, and keep in mind that a moral wrong is wrong, regardless of its size."

"I didn't get that thing about trans . . . trans . . . trans . . . Umm . . ."

"Transcendental consequences," Lucia coached.

"Yeah, transcendental consequences." Alfonso could not believe he was so caught up in this very heady discussion and was feeling very smart.

"Good question. The word *transcendental* is the concept of *transcending*, or climbing, going beyond. As when you finished elementary school, you were able to go further, beyond, to middle school. You were able to do this as a consequence of challenges transcended positively. You were able to climb the ladder to success! This is a very simplified example of a complex concept, but I hope you got the picture."

Lucia looked him over, noticed his fatigue, and said, "Look, Alfonso, the bottom line is, behave well, and don't give your poor mother unnecessary headaches."

Alfonso nodded, sucked hard on his straw, and enjoyed the noisy sound of the last bit of milk shake. Lucia touched the screen of her cell phone to call Adele to come get them. "Remember what I told you, Alfonso," she advised, "or you will have to sit through this lecture all over again."

Alfonso smiled weakly.

"And no more robbing convenience stores."

Alfonso felt himself nearly faint.

"Adele!" Lucia said, "We're ready to be picked up."

10

Accident or Miracle

L UCIA SPENT A few peaceful days watering her violets, catching up with politics from her accumulated newspapers, and going to the movies with her family. All except her husband, that is. Gary preferred to comfortably change channels on his television. One late afternoon, looking at her watch, she realized that she had plenty time to walk to the Ocho for a scoop of her favorite pistachio ice cream. After that nice walk, she chuckled to herself. *I will certainly have earned the right to enjoy all those delicious calories,* she thought. With a childlike grin of anticipation, she set off for her treat.

Arriving at the ice cream parlor, a small group of young people there who recognized her joyfully greeted her. She knew a few of them by name—Caesar, David, and Helen. They made room for her at their table so they could talk to her. One of the young folks asked, "Professor, did you hear about Julie's accident?"

"No, I did not realize she'd been in an accident! Please tell me what happened to her. My god, she is only fourteen years old! Is she okay?"

"Imagine the worst, Professor. Julie's mother had an accident driving her car across that narrow bridge on Route 7, and Julie was with her."

"I have always said that bridge is extremely dangerous!" said Lucia.

A young man in the group named Paul added, "As Julie's mother drove across the bridge, there was a large semi in the oncoming lane. To avoid scraping vehicles, she drove too closely to the right side of the bridge. The car door scraped the side of the bridge so badly that it ripped off! Unfortunately, Julie was in the front passenger seat and was not wearing her seat belt, so when the door broke off, she flew out!"

"What did her poor mother do when she realized what had happened? What did the truck driver do?" the professor quickly peppered the young man with urgent questions.

"Well, the truck driver was oblivious and continued across the bridge unaware of the tragedy that had just occurred," Paul said. "Julie's mother stopped her car immediately, jumped out, and ran around screaming for help, frantically searching for her daughter."

"That particular bridge," said Lucia, "is so high above the river that you nearly see the top of the trees along the edge of the water."

"I know," Paul said. "Julie's mother was frantic. Several cars actually did stop to help her, and within minutes, the police and emergency crew were there."

As Paul continued to fill in the story, the professor learned that many feared Julie had fallen into the river and already been taken by the current. It was springtime, so the water was high, and the currents ran deep and fast. The main fear, of course, was that Julie drowned.

Paul's eyes burned brightly as he related what happened next. "Within minutes of arriving on the bank of the river, one of the paramedics looked up, and there in the branches of a tree, he saw Julie! It was unbelievable, a miracle! Julie had plenty of bruises and scrapes, but she was alive."

Relieved that the young lady was rescued, Lucia got up to buy her nearly forgotten pistachio ice-cream cone. When she returned to the table of young folks, Caesar posed a question. At this point in his life, Caesar, one of the regulars at Kat's Café and frequent attendee of the professor's Saturday lectures, was more agnostic than religious.

"What would you call Julie's incident, an accident or a miracle?" he asked. The group was equally divided on the question. There were those who agreed that it was simply an accident, but David spoke up, saying he heard that there were those at the scene who said that when Julie was flying from her car, an angel swooped in, grabbed her, and placed her in the tree.

"Just a moment," said Lucia. "Let's first clarify our terms. What is an accident, and what is a miracle? If Boethius, a fifth-century Roman senator and great thinker, could weigh in on the subject, he would say that an accident is a very unfortunate event whose cause we don't understand, and a miracle is a wonderful and happy effect whose cause we don't understand either.

"Have you also noticed how when we experience an unfortunate event, we always wonder how such a horrible thing could have been avoided?"

Helen, who had been so attentive of Lucia's words that she turned off her cell phone, said, "You know, you're right on. I'm sure all of us are thinking of ways we could have avoided that situation. If that had been me, I would have insisted that Julie wear her seat belt."

Someone else said that he wouldn't have taken that dangerous bridge route, and another said that she would have known better than to move too far to the right like Julie's mother had.

"Okay, that's enough of all of the useless rhetoric of 'I would have' or 'If I had or had not.' This kind of thinking uses the most neurotic expressions in the English language. That way of thinking is totally absurd because no one can unwind the clock, go back to the past, and change what has already happened." Lucia, while blunt, maintained a tone of kindness.

"I tell you what," said Lucia. "Let's order another round of ice cream on me. Then let's see if we can't make some sense of the difference between accidents and miracles."

Happily enjoying their treats, the group continued to probe the professor's mind.

"It is clear that accidents occur all the time. But, Professor, what about miracles? Miracles like the birth of a baby," asked Helen.

"Yes, like a birth of a baby, of course!" she agreed. "But," the professor continued, "concerning accidents, we should do two things: follow Plato's advice to take our time to *think before we act* and make sure to put into practice Aristotle's formula of the Four Rights. Do you remember them from one of my Saturday lectures?" All around the students smiled and shrugged in embarrassed ignorance.

"Well, in this case, it means that when we drive, it is very important to drive the *right* car, at the *right* speed, on the *right* road, and for the *right* reason. The four *rights*. Remember?" Now the students nodded in recognition. Lucia went on, "On the other hand, do you remember Aesop's fable of Hercules and the Waggoner? The gods help those who help themselves?"

"Yes, but who is ever lucky enough to get that divine help?" challenged Caesar, the agnostic. "Is it that sometimes we have it and other times we don't?

"Don't you think," said Lucia, "that if we tell Julie to consider herself lucky, she could also say that she would be better off if she had not had any accident at all? But if we ask the same question of her mother, she would say that the fact that her daughter survived the accident was miracle. So, are accidents necessary? Of course, they are not. But are there also any miracles? Yes, there are, but in order to experience them, it is important to put in practice our divine reason. That is to say, calculate before we act, and pay attention to what we are doing, especially while driving."

Caesar softly repeated to himself, "Divine reason, divine reason," as if he were learning some foreign terminology and forcing the idea beyond his skepticism.

"You have made a good point, Professor," said Helen. "In addition to causing a terrible accident, Julie's mom got a costly ticket because her child was not wearing her seat belt."

"That's right, Helen. We can all learn from this empirical lesson and make sure we wear our seat belts, right?"

"Empiric what?" asked Mr. Washington from behind the counter as he turned the main lights off, casting the room into blue shadows.

"I am so glad you asked, Mr. Washington, because you are asking for everyone, I'm sure. Empirical lesson or empirical moment means that we can learn from others' experiences. Very well, my dear friends, there is now empirical evidence that the shop is closing. Didn't any of you notice that the lights are out? Good night one and all."

"Professor," offered Caesar, "would you like a ride home?"

"Thank you, Caesar, but if I walk home, I will be happy about having a double ice cream, but if I do not walk it off, I will be lamenting my indulgence." She patted her belly to reinforce the thought.

"Of course, Professor," Caesar said, "some other time."

"On the other hand," said Lucia, "why don't you give Helen a ride? It has gotten dark and rather late."

Helen smiled shyly, silently grateful that Lucia surely had noticed her crush on Caesar.

"Good idea. Good night, and thank you for the ice cream," said Caesar.

When Lucia arrived home, her husband, Gary, called from the kitchen. He had whipped up chicken enchiladas in salsa verde for their dinner. Lucia briefly considered stuffing half of one down to show her appreciation, then ultimately confessed to having had two scoops of ice cream. Gary laughed, gave her a hug, and said he'd eat in front of the TV. He told her he put her mail on her desk.

Lucia went into her home office and stood at her desk, shuffling mail and smiling as she recognized a letter sent to her by Patricia, an old and dear friend of hers. She set it aside to read the next day. She was tired and so looking forward to putting her head down on her pillow. Ah, blessed sleep!

11

What Could Have Been . . .

A FTER A GOOD night's sleep, Lucia sat in the cozy kitchen, enjoying a hot mug of strong coffee. She usually read the paper with her coffee, but this morning, she opened the letter from Patricia. Now that she was rested, she could give it her full, undivided attention.

My dearest professor and trusted friend,

My father has died. I weep, but not because he has died, but rather for what he could have been but never was.

Your loyal student and friend,
Patricia

Lucia read Patricia's letter again, then swiftly got out paper and pen and wrote:

My dearest Patricia,

One of the most unavoidable and heartbreaking circumstances that we can ever experience, not just once, but often several times during our lifetime, is the death of a relative or friend.

Today, in your letter, you tell me about your father's death. How can I console you? How can I help you endure this grief?

Typically one says, "I am so sorry for your loss; he was such a wonderful man; may God have him on his right side," or "time will heal you."

I had all those thoughts when I read your sad news, but I don't really want to use any of those words. I prefer to help you understand what you yourself wrote. You say that you cry, not because he died, but rather for what he could have been but never was.

My dearest Patricia, I have always thought of you as a person of genuine sentiments. What you have said is your most intimate truth concerning the pain your father's death has produced in you.

When you learned of his death, you cried because his soul had left this earth. But the reality is that in your heart you have felt that, since the last time you saw him (more than twenty years ago, your father's soul was already gone.

Unfortunately, during your upbringing, your father had lost his sense of responsibility toward his children. He was too self-involved and egocentric. We will never know what kind of childhood experiences he had that made him as hard as iron and as tough as a general. Oddly, he had the capability to be kind, charming, and even romantic enough to conquer your mother's heart, although seemingly for his own convenience.

Sadly, once they married, once she was his, he became a miserable despot.

As you know, your mother was in love with him for reasons only she understands. For many years, she was quite compliant and did exactly what your father demanded of her.

But over time she became very wise. Your mother knew that as long as she complied with your father's wishes because he made a decent living, she and the children would have a secure, comfortable life. However, it was inevitable that even comfortable security wasn't enough to compensate for being under his thumb, so she eventually divorced him.

She had felt that being married to your father was like having a terrible virus that was slowing leaching joy out of her and your lives. By her leaving him, you all began living a healthier, happier life.

I know you well enough to say that you are the one child, out of five, who was, and still is, closest to your mother. You, my dear, have a very clear and healthy mind, so your awareness of your mother's situation made it quite personal for you. You felt the anguish your father's treatment of your mother caused her in an intensely painful way.

That said, let me now address what you wrote about what your father never was. You say this because the pain and emotional suffering you experienced as a child kept you from having a full and loving relationship with him as you progressed in your own life with its experiences of education, marriage, and motherhood.

You had even chosen to withhold your own children from their grandfather because, in truth, your father has always seemed more dead than alive to you. Now, he is gone, and you no longer have a problem, no more doubt, uncertainty, or difficulty in need of a solution regarding your relationship with him. You now have only a situation. Your father's role in your life was of critical significance. Now that he is gone, you can move forward.

It is delightful to see your solid and resolute personality. Some people are like badly paved city roads that always have potholes. They patch and repatch the holes, but the road is always bad. You are not one of these people!

For you to stay strong, it is best to believe your father has found tranquility of spirit, the tranquility he was unable to attain in his lifetime.

Heraclitus, an ancient philosopher, used to have his students stand ankle-deep in a shallow river, facing upstream. He told them to look behind them without moving their feet. He'd point out that the water would become muddy from the slight movement of turning the head to look back.

His idea was that in looking backward instead of forward in life, things become unclear to us. We lose sight of the never-ending freshness of life. Every molecule of water, just like every second of life, is present, passes by, then it's gone, constantly replaced by another and another.

Let's apply this to your life, my dearest friend. Heraclitus would say, "The water that touches me now will never touch me again." You need to enjoy the metaphor: find new rivers, walk in, and face the source of the stream. Plant your feet and face forward, allowing the water of life to wash over you, refreshing and nourishing. Don't muddy your life by looking back and wondering what could have been. That is neurotic and definitely not your style.

And, as always, keep that cheerful personality of yours! It seems to me that, thanks to your mother, you were born smiling.

Take care of yourself, my dear Patricia and, as always,

With love,
Lucia

12

Temperance or Moderation

T HE DAY OF Lucia's visit to the ice cream parlor, one of the young women, Helen, became so involved with the story of Julie's accident and Lucia's conversation that she turned off her cell phone because friends kept calling and interrupting. Of course, Helen's mother phoned right after that; the call went to voice mail, so she phoned again—many times. Not being able to reach her daughter made Mrs. Jones extremely upset.

When Helen came home, her mother was furious. "Helen, for heaven's sake, don't ever do that again!" her mother cried.

"But what did I do?" replied Helen.

"What did you do? You had me praying for hours! I prayed to all the saints! I actually thought I would die not knowing why you weren't answering your phone! I was certain something horrible had happened to you." While Helen's mother was shouting, crying and carrying on, Helen felt removed from the drama of her mother's emotion. She had only one thought: how could she get her mother over to Professor Lucia's so she could help her find some balance?

"Mom, I am so sorry to have caused you so much anxiety," Helen said.

"Where on earth were you?" her mother demanded.

Helen told her that she was at the Ocho with friends, enjoying listening to the professor discuss accidents and miracles. She said Caesar drove her home, which brought more howls.

Her mother was still upset and told Helen that she certainly could have called her to say she was safe. What she didn't tell her daughter was that she did not believe her excuse. That the boy Caesar drove her home confirmed the idea in her mind that Helen was not at the ice cream parlor but up to monkey business. But she kept that idea to herself.

It was clear to Helen though that her mother was skeptical. Helen gave her a hug, apologized one more time, and then went to her room, determined to call the professor first thing in the morning.

Typical of the professor, when Helen asked for her help the next day, she agreed immediately to go by her house that afternoon. Lucia was well acquainted with the irrational character of the excessively worried mother. Her own mother had been one of those.

As a young woman, she did her best to be home on time, but when she was unable to do so, all she could ever do was to apologize. But when she was late and no one had missed her, then she wouldn't say a word. To her that was like handing ammunition to the enemy. If she wasn't being missed as much as she expected, why point out that she was late? That way no one would then be able to throw that in her face any time in the future, and she sure didn't want to hear "you're always late" for the rest of her life. Helen's mom wasn't going to be a challenge for Lucia.

That afternoon, Lucia went to see Helen's mother at her house. Mrs. Jones greeted her with a great deal of affection and deference.

"Professor," she said, gushing, "What a delight to see you. Please come in. What brings you to my neck of the woods?"

"I was heading to the flower shop, and it occurred to me that I hadn't seen you in well over a month, so here I am," announced Lucia. "Are you free for a few minutes?"

"But of course I am. You are always welcome in my home, Professor. I'll put on a pot of coffee. Come, make yourself comfortable," she said, leading her into the cozy kitchen. "I must confess, Lucia," said Mrs. Jones, "that I woke up this morning with you on my mind. I was thinking about how whenever I attend one of your lectures at Kat's Café, I leave with knowledge that is not only applicable to my life but is also therapeutic!"

"That's great to hear. So how have you been?"

"Well, actually, there is something really bothering me today. Perhaps I could share it with you?"

The professor smiled gently and assured her that nothing would please her more than to be of assistance. Mrs. Jones launched into her saga, telling her of becoming a total basket case the night before.

"I thought I was going to have an anxiety attack when I could not reach Helen last night. I called and called, but she never answered her phone. I was sure something horrible had befallen her!"

"Ah," said the professor, "Helen was at the Ocho with me last night. I do recall seeing her turn off her phone. We were having a wonderful time, so she probably just didn't want any interruptions. How unfortunate for you however."

Mrs. Jones hoped to catch Helen in a lie. She wanted to blame her for all the anxiety she suffered, but at the same time, she was thoroughly embarrassed to find that her daughter had not lied. She looked at Professor Lucia sheepishly.

"I can't believe I actually hoped that I could blame Helen for my own hysteria. Perhaps you could help me make some sense of my emotions, Lucia?"

"It is certainly normal for a mother to experience anxiety about her child. But perhaps it would help to know that you don't need to suffer so much. You just need to practice *temperance*. There are other words for this, such as self-control, equilibrium, or emotional balance."

"I thought I did have self control. Are you telling me I don't?"

"You're probably familiar with the New Year's song, "Auld Lang Syne"? It was written by the poet Robert Burns, who also wrote, 'O if some power the Good Lord give us / To see ourselves as others see us.' I rely on my husband Gary to tell me when I'm doing something I don't realize that I should be aware of. But enough of me. You see, practicing *temperance* is spiritual but can also be physiological. Take eating. Now, to me you appear very slim and fit. So you must apply *temperance*, which results in eating *moderately*, not excessively. The benefits of eating moderately are that it is good for one's health, provides a sense of self-worth, and the cumulative effect is a longer, more robust life. Moderation in all things, physical, psychological, spiritual, or behavioral, it all adds up to the same thing: a more peaceful life.

"Now in your case, you need a paradigm shift to temper your consideration of your daughter's actions. When Helen turned off her phone, two observations were created. Helen observed that we could all concentrate on our philosophical discussion without the distraction of her phone ringing. On the other hand, being unable to communicate with her made you crazy, imagining disastrous scenarios of harm coming to your daughter.

"Now, imagine a thermometer that measures temperance. Can you visualize it?" Mrs. Jones nodded. "Okay, now imagine that you can see it measuring Helen's temperance and then yours. What I see is that

Helen's temperance measures just the right degree. Yours, on the other hand, pops the mercury all the way to the top of the thermometer!"

Mrs. Jones's jaw dropped slightly. She recalled the feeling of blowing her top, much like Lucia's image of the thermometer.

"Practicing temperance is calming," Lucia added. "For instance, let's imagine a husband who finds his wife still in bed while he's trying to get the children off to school, make his own lunch, and get ready for work. He eventually blows up at her. He screams that she is the laziest person on the face of the earth. However, he can also temper his anger and show kindness and concern for his wife by saying, 'My goodness, my dear, are you feeling okay?'" said the Lucia, "You can see how beneficial the application of temperance could be, am I right?"

Mrs. Jones nodded in agreement. "I can see that as far as your example of the husband goes, but I have a bigger problem. My imagination gets carried away when my children are out and about at night. As you well know, young people have no fear. They think that they are invincible. But you and I know differently. So if they are not home on time, I imagine all kinds of awful things happening to them, and I feel responsible for them."

"Then let me give you something to think about," Lucia suggested, "that will help you put your worries in perspective. In the eighteenth century, a British philosopher named David Hume postulated that knowledge comes from the impressions of all our experiences, whether actual or from our imagination. Our mind can access these images at will, and even imagined mental ideas can feel real under the right circumstances. One has to be very careful not to confuse the two. Think about this idea: Let's say you hear a noise outside. You would swear it sounds like hoofbeats pounding on the pavement outside your house. When you run to the window to see what's happening, do you expect to see zebras? I don't think so because that's not likely to be the case, unless you are living in Africa. No, you most certainly would be expecting to see horses, not zebras. Note that I said expecting because that's the mental image that your experience would provide to match the sound of hoofbeats.

"When your kids are late," she continued, "what mental images do you conjure up? Where do they come from? What can you realistically expect? Nine hundred ninety-nine chances out of a thousand, they are on their way home safely, only slightly delayed. The chance they have been run down by marauding zebras is virtually nonexistent. Can you see how tempering your imagination would help you to expect nothing unusual to have happened?"

"When you put it like that, it just makes sense. Thanks so much. I get now that *temperance means restraint, self-control, and equanimity.* I can do that!" Mrs. Jones beamed.

"I'll give you one more concept to think about, as long as we are on this subject. When you put *temperance* into practice, you are actually practicing something called *logo therapy*. This term, coined by Victor Frankl, a twentieth-century neurologist and psychotherapist, means putting into practice holding only healthy thoughts. It's existentialism at its very best because it emphasizes the freedom of the will and the consequent responsibility of this notion. If you have only corrosive thoughts in your mind, these ill thoughts will pollute your soul. But you can become your own therapist, capable of bringing about your own mental health.

"But enough of this for now, my dear. I certainly am delighted I happened to come by today. I'll just finish my coffee and then be on my way." The professor smiled at her over the steaming mug, delighted to observe that Mrs. Jones was visibly more relaxed.

"Join us sometime at Kat's. Every third Saturday," Lucia offered.

"Maybe I will," said Mrs. Jones. "If only to keep an eye on Helen."

Ayayay, thought Lucia. *Teaching is hard.*

13

Childhood: Comprehension or Mistreatment?

A COUPLE OF weeks went by, and Lucia continued her personal routine without crossing the path of anyone needing philosophical advice. Lucia took advantage of those isolated opportunities to finish some of her projects, including the regular six-month visit to her dentist and her annual physical. She went to the movies with Glynis, her former student and by now her friend and movie partner. For Lucia, going to the movies was akin to walking into Plato's cave, allowing all the images projected on the screen to come alive for her, knowing that they were "colorful shadows" on the wall. Even so, she could not help but think those beguiling shadows can rob us of our cognitive ability, making us feel excessive joy, nostalgia, love, and loyalty for the handsome star that is about to get caught, but he is so good at his corruptive craft that he deserves to win. Lucia also enjoyed her soda and buttered popcorn.

Then the third Saturday of the month arrived, and that meant a visit to Kat's Café Lucia and her once-a-month philosophical discussion. On this particular Saturday, Lucia made sure the public meeting posting invited young parents because she intended to dedicate this talk to the raising of healthy children.

Her regulars and five or six curious young couples met and mingled. The first moments of greetings were followed by coffee and refreshments, and Beatriz milled about offering her homemade cookies. Lucia held small chats here and there until there was enough audience for her to begin her Saturday talk.

"Good evening, dear friends," Kat announced. "It is a pleasure to introduce you one more time to my dear friend, Señora Lucia."

After the polite applause died down, Lucia said, "*Muchas gracias*, Kat. You are always so kind to let us use this magnificent space here in your café." She stood tall and strong and, for a moment, looked silently over her expectant audience, a technique she had intuitively learned to command attention.

"Today I want to talk to you about one very important period of our lives, childhood. As you may know, as small children become capable of using full sentences when they speak, a lot of parents begin to treat them as if they are not that small anymore. Plato, one of my favorite thinkers of all time, suggests that first lessons taught to the children one should use fiction. There is no need to have them grow up so quickly.

"Yes!" a young woman exclaimed. All attention turned to her. She felt compelled to add, "You are so right."

"Thank you," Lucia said. "Can you introduce yourself and keep going and tell us what you mean?"

Fighting embarrassment, the young woman said, "Irene. Irene Tobolowsky. I do everything possible to keep my little boy a child, but his dad treats him as if he were an adult already."

Murmuring of recognition rose. Lucia asked, "Irene, could you give us an example?"

Irene nodded. "The other day in McDonald's, my boy had to go to the restroom. He's only three. My husband barely looked up from his iPad and told him to go by himself, and "When you finish, make sure to wash your hands." When Jimmy—that's my son—tried to get my husband to go with him, my husband said, 'You're old enough to do that by yourself.'"

Lucia shrugged. "I don't see anything wrong with that, so long as it was a safe place."

"Okay then, but what about when one of us has to leave to go to work or something. Jimmy acts devastated."

"This is one of the reasons why I tell all the parents that it is very important to use fiction while talking to the little children. Engage their imagination. You can take the child to the world of fantasy. When either of you have to leave, give Jimmy something to focus on that inspires his imagination. However, be very careful not to deceive the children with false promises," Lucia advised.

"It is important to come down to the children's level and allow them to paint their own landscapes using their imagination. The adults need to know that the children's ideas take their time going through the *rational filters.*"

A young couple exchanged confused glances, and the husband spoke up, "We don't know what you mean by *rational filters*."

"Good that you asked me," Lucia said. "This is a concept that I have reinterpreted from the *Critique of Pure Reason*, a book by Immanuel Kant, the most important philosopher of the eighteenth century. From Kant's point of view, the child reasons, but reason at this level is only a tool like a pair of pliers that hold the idea. With those pliers, the child holds those ideas in his mind as if the idea were already a perfect reality because the idea is already part of his imaginary world. Our task is to help the child pass that idea through the filters of comprehension. For children that speak 'clearly and distinctly,' it can be more difficult for us to believe they need correction because they have strong verbal skills."

Grace, a regular, raised her hand. "Lucia, I had an interesting experience the other day when I went to visit my little nephew." Lucia motioned for her to go ahead. "Well, I opened the refrigerator door in front of my nephew and pulled the vegetable drawer out, and he saw what to him were two green balls. I had to explain to him that they were limes and not balls, but he insisted that they were balls. So I made some limeade. He watched closely while I cut the limes, juiced them, and added sugar and water, and then he drank a full glass. After that I took him to his toy box to look for two balls, and fortunately, there were a couple of green ones. And I asked him if he thought we could make limeade from those, and he said, "No. That's crazy. These are *balls*!" Appreciative chuckles came from the others.

"Wonderful Grace, what you did helped your nephew to pass the idea from his reason to his comprehension successfully. Empathy is other psychological tool that can help us reach the imaginary world of children, and by empathy, I mean, the ability to see the world from another's point of view. When your nephew said that the limes were balls, you could begin by giving him credit for the similarity between limes and balls."

A tall, young professional man spoke up next. "Jason Markham. This is my wife Jenna. In the beginning, you said that it is very important not to think that the children are older when they are not. In our case, all our children are very tall, and everybody thinks they're, like, three or four years older than they are, and that's very rough for them. How do we help with that?"

Lucia thought. "Children never mind telling their age. And they are perceptive when someone makes that incorrect assumption. Encourage them to tell people their age. That will help the adult correct their misconception." The couple thanked her and sat back.

Lucia thought it a good time to announce a break, but before she could, one of the single mothers demanded. "What about punishment for the children?"

"Punishment? That is a big word. It can be part of a discipline formula. Do you have a specific question?"

The young mother said, "My name is Dolores, and I have four children—twin girls age eight, a boy age five, and a girl age two.

"How wonderful! Just like me, three girls and one boy." Lucia smiled.

"The other day while the twins were playing, they started to argue and fight. I didn't know and didn't care who started it, so I sent them both to sit in the living room for an hour. That was torture for me, and that was the longest hour of my life. What can I do next time?"

"Well, it is recommended with the famous 'time-out' to put in practice a minute for each year they are old. So an hour was excessive. Your girls would have been fine with no more than ten minutes, and they would have experienced a very applicable punishment." Lucia heard a tall, cool ice tea calling her name, so before anyone else jumped in, she segued, "But speaking of 'time-out', let's take a few minutes to stretch our legs and maybe have more of those delicious cookies and coffee."

After everyone had gotten more refreshments, Lucia continued. "Earlier, I spoke of when children are capable of reason. According to psychologists, children begin to reason no earlier than age seven. When you tell a child of three to five or six years of age, 'If you don't behave, I am not going to buy you any toys,' you can't be surprised if the child answers, 'I don't care. I already have plenty of toys.' The child knows that there is some kind of fighting challenge, and she is going to try to win. That's all."

"So then, how can we make the child obey?" asked another of the young mothers.

"In measuring the punishment, make sure to select the kind of *punishment* for which *you* can survive the *consequences*. Many times, parents select too severe a punishment, so severe that they have to forgive the child, not because the kid deserves forgiveness, but because the parent can't sweat the consequences of the chosen punishment. Like your famous hour of torture, Dolores, though you held out. But the other impetus is to forgive to take the pressure off yourself. And what happens? The child that was forgiven just won another war. And don't ever send the child to his room, especially if there is a television in that room. By the way, what did all of us from the last century do since we had no TV? We played, we ran, we collected insects, and all sorts of activities."

"That was a different time," Jason stated. "You can't let kids play unsupervised. They'd kill themselves or get kidnapped or worse."

"There is a certain amount of danger in an urban environment, I agree. But, you know, I have friends your age who grew up in Manhattan and in Mexico City, and they played unsupervised in parks and on sidewalks, and you know what? They survived! Now, I completely understand your concern, but teach your children basic safety—don't talk to strangers, don't run into the street—and I'll bet they survive too. I wonder if being overprotective is one of the causes of childhood obesity. Please let the children play!" There were murmurs again, this time not in complete agreement.

"Plato suggested talking to the children with fiction or metaphors. Aesop created little stories—fables—that had specific behavior concepts called 'morals' explicitly stated. Some, like "The Boy Who Cried Wolf" are cautionary tales, effective in teaching the cause and effect of actions. And there is much other literature to aid in helping children learn positive behaviors. A good source is the website for the Newberry Award for the best in children's literature. Of course, children's librarians are exceptionally knowledgeable and can recommend books that address many behavioral issues. The bottom line, my dear friends, is when the child grows up without witnessing violence, adult temper tantrums, and foul language, he becomes a decent and happy adult. We must help children enjoy their constitutional rights to 'life, liberty and the pursuit of happiness.' And we must keep in mind that we must not break promises. When the child hears, 'When we get home, I'll give you an ice cream,' the grown-up may just say it to make the child happy for the moment, but for the child, that promise will stay alive for the longest time."

Dolores spoke up again, "I was told by my daughter's kindergarten teacher that during 'sharing time,' my girl, crying, told the class her saddest day ever was the day my husband promised to take her to McDonald's but never did. I sat her down and told her that a missed trip to McDonald's was not worth crying over."

"But for her, it was. It wasn't the missed trip for a Happy Meal. It was experiencing betrayal by the person she trusted most," Lucia explained. "Yes, this seems simple to you, and indeed it is simple, but what we must learn is that children very quickly move their learning experiences from 'simple to complex' ideas, as John Locke explains it in his treatise *The Ideas of Human Understanding,* written all the way back in the eighteenth century. The simple ideas are concrete—toy, candy, milk, dog. The complex ideas are abstract—goodness, trust, belief, promises, love, confidence. Your daughter was able to keep in her tender heart disillusionment when her dad betrayed her by not fulfilling his promises.

"With time, if the child experiences nothing but broken promises, he or she may grow up to be fearful, nervous, doubtful, insecure, and resentful whenever someone makes a promise. Thus, this poor child grows up to be one with a very difficult personality. Let's understand how our actions—commissions and omissions—affect our beloved children in order to help them be happy adults because this is our most serious civic and ethical responsibility." Lucia relaxed her posture and said, "Let's stop our discussion here and meet again next month." The group surrounded her immediately, peppering her with questions until Kat stepped in and closed the café.

14

Mechanical Philosophy

T HERE WAS NO sound. Actually, there were plenty of sounds from cars passing on the street, just not the one Lucia wanted to hear: that of her car starting. When she tried the ignition, there was not even a click.

The day had started so well. A light rain fell, freshening the stale air, and Lucia drove downtown to join a teaching colleague for coffee. Now this: after a long discussion of Hegel during which time got away from her, she came out midafternoon, and her car refused to do what she expected it to do. At least, she thought, I'm in a daylong parking space in the lot, and I won't get a ticket on top of this.

She called Charlie the mechanic on her cell phone, and he said he would be right down to help. Waiting for him in the now sunny afternoon, Lucia thought, *I often wonder how we survived all of those years without the cell phone. Now it is another organ as important as the liver or the kidneys or even the heart.*

Charlie rolled up in his tow truck, said a quick hello, popped the hood on Lucia's car, and hooked up a pair of cables to the battery. "Try it now," he told her. The car started up immediately.

"Wonderful!" exclaimed Lucia. "What do I owe you?"

"It's not over yet," Charlie replied. "Turn your lights off, then follow me back to the shop. You ran your battery down. I have to put it on the charger."

With Lucia's battery hooked to the charger in the garage, Charlie came back into the waiting area. His mechanics, Manny, Juan, and Tojo, worked steadily on other cars in the sparkling clean facility. Lucia asked, "So, Charlie, tell me what is new with you."

Charlie finished wiping his hands and replied, "Don't even start."

"For heaven's sakes, Charlie, anyone would say that by your tone of voice you need to recharge your spiritual battery. What happened to your spark?"

"Well, Lucia, you nearly hit the nail on the head," Charlie said. He picked up a small stack of work orders and sorted.

Lucia observed he seemed to work hard at focusing on the papers to avoid talking to her. She went to the coffeemaker in the corner Charlie provided for customers, poured a cup, and passed it under Charlie's nose, teasing, "Coffee, Charlie . . . coffee." He looked up, mildly irritated. "Come on, Charlie, speak up. What's bugging you?"

"You seriously want to know, or do you want me to say I have a toothache or something?"

"I seriously want to know. Unless you really do have a toothache, and then I'll say get to a dentist. But I suspect it has to do with your spiritual battery. Now, take this coffee and I'll pour one for myself."

He motioned her to his tiny office, and they sat down and sipped. "Lucia," he said, "You and me, we've known each other a long time."

"Decades."

"Yeah. Decades. Well, as you know, I have a lot of relatives, and when they need me, they sure come to see me. I talk to them, give them advice, and I even lend them or give them money. Then they leave, and I feel as if, after all of that, we didn't even connect."

Lucia took his hand and softly advised, "Dear friend, my suggestion for you is that when you go out of your way to advise them and even given them money, don't wait for them to show you any gratitude, but instead, focus on the *intention* of your giving. Your intention is to help keep them going, just as a charged battery keeps a car going. When the battery of the car gives energy to the starter motor and then the car starts, we don't thank the battery. Instead, we are grateful the car runs. Your friends and relatives are deeply grateful. Trust me on this."

"I guess," Charlie sighed.

"Hey. You immediately knew my car battery needed charging. You told me that when the battery is low, the car begins to fail. I'm telling you that your own battery is awfully low. I sense that you are disillusioned and not necessarily happy, but if you don't find the remedy and charge your spiritual battery, you may begin to experience a meaningless existence, apathy, and lethargy."

"Apathy and lethargy, what are those? Sounds like a law firm." Charlie attempted to deflect with some humor, but Lucia did not pause. "Allow me to explain those two terms the same way that Miguel de Unamuno, the great Spanish thinker of the turn of the century, did."

"Who?"

"Here's a little story about me. The first thesis I wrote for my masters in philosophy was about Miguel de Unamuno."

"Wait," Charlie interrupted. "What do you mean your first thesis? Do you need to write more than one?"

"Give me a second," Lucia admonished. "There's more to this story. My first thesis burned."

"You were that unhappy with it?"

"Ha!" she laughed. "It was probably the most brilliant, most insightful piece of philosophical research ever written."

"Really," Charlie replied, uncertain if Lucia was teasing or delusional.

"Since it's gone, we'll never know, will we? No, I didn't burn my thesis, not with all the work I put into it. During that time in graduate school, I roomed with my sister and her family. You know children and matches, the worst combination ever and even worse if one is a pyromaniac. My little nephew's friend was one of those. My room was his fourth fire."

Charlie sighed. "I understand what you must have felt. All that work gone. I would have been depressed for months."

"You know, Charlie. As a matter of fact, I actually remember my first thoughts after that fire. I remember thinking, well, this is a moment of truth because what I have truly learned is in my head, and what I thought I knew is now only ashes. But I did graduate by writing another thesis that actually changed my outlook in life. We can talk about that another time. My point is I took something that could have, as you say, depressed me for weeks and instead recharged my spiritual battery and accomplished something that had more effect on me. Enough of that. Let's find out why your own battery is so low."

Charlie had about enough of this. With everything else in his life, he didn't need a preacher in his business, lording a how-to-live-your-life-right sermon over him. "Let's see if your battery is ready to come off the charger," he said, getting up.

"Hang on a minute," she said, stopping him. Any time Lucia crossed the path of someone like Charlie, she would always keep in mind how Socrates was able to help a young illiterate man solve a trigonometry problem by drawing in the sand with a stick using the tools and understanding of the young man. She quickly adapted to explain using experiences Charlie already comprehended. "You like TV, don't you?"

He sighed loudly. Playing along, he said, "Yeah, I like TV."

"What are your favorite shows?"

"Football. *American Idol. Orange County Choppers*."

"Besides reality, what do you like?"

Charlie thought. "*Breaking Bad. Law and Order*."

"All right. Drama," Lucia agreed. "Let's talk about drama and the philosopher Unamuno. Unamuno wrote more than ten thousand pages of drama and poetry and only one book of philosophy, titled *The Tragic Sense of Life*.

"That's a gloomy title."

"Gloomy indeed, Charlie, but that book explains the danger of walking into the life of idleness, lethargy, apathy, and nothingness. You would never read a book like that, would you?" Charlie shook his head. "I think Unamuno suspected that too, so he wrote a dramatic novel to explain the evil evolved in any of those choices. The title is *The Fog*, and the main character is named August."

"Not Charlie, then?" Charlie smiled, knowing how Lucia liked to slant things.

"Not Charlie," Lucia continued, oblivious. "Well, August is a single, healthy, rich, and spoiled man who, thanks to his rich parents, has everything he desires yet nothing to do, and not having anything to do, he begins to experience lethargy, laziness, and apathy. Because he has everything, there are never any challenges for miserable August.

"With all of that money," Charlie said, "he could come to me and I would have given him a handful of good ideas—for a good payment, of course."

Now Lucia sighed, took a breath, and continued. "So one morning he wakes up incredibly excited because he finally found a reason for his existence. He now has the project of his lifetime!" she exclaimed.

"And what in God's name is his project?" Charlie mocked.

"And August said, 'I know what I am going to do! I am going to kill myself!'"

"What?" Charlie stated, puzzled and suddenly let down. "Was he nuts? Did he have a screw loose?"

Satisfied she had his attention, Lucia said excitedly, "But wait. In the next moment, Unamuno, as the writer, jumps on the page of the novel and says, "*Un momentito*! One moment young man! You may not kill yourself because I am your father. I have given you birth. I have given you the life you have, and I do not allow you to kill yourself."

MARÍA ELENA PELLINEN

Charlie frowned. A writer putting himself in his own novel and talking directly to a character he created. "I was with you for a minute, Lucia, but this? This is crazy time."

"What Unamuno is trying to do for August is recharge the battery of his existence because he is on his way to a very bad depression. Just like Unamuno, I don't want to see you catching that sick bug."

"So now I'm one of your creations?" Charlie made a little whistle and rotated his index finger next to his head.

"Of course, you're not one of my creations," Lucia apologized, realizing she might have been a bit high handed. "What I'm saying is you still have plenty of spark, and your engine is running quite well. You take care of recharging my car battery while I take care of recharging your soul battery."

"You're not suggesting a trade, are you? Because I'm already traded for plumbing and landscaping. I can't afford another trade, not if my employees expect to be paid."

"I'll pay you, Charlie. Don't sweat that. You have enough people taking advantage of your good will. That's what you've been telling me. You see, when you have expectations of people, that means that you anticipate that certain things will be done by the people who you have just helped. Perhaps while you advise your relatives, you think that they are going to do exactly what you suggest because why wouldn't they? But then they don't! And then you suffer emotional exertion that wipes out more energy from you than one week of doing car mechanics."

"You got that right, Lucia," Charlie agreed.

"I understand. This is where I can hopefully give you some practical advice. Let me show you how to apply the best of the emotional mechanics in philosophy named phenomenology."

"Fee-name . . . Let's go see about that battery."

"Phe-no-me-no-lo-gy, the branch of philosophy that teaches you to suspend all your experiences, just as you can stop a DVD then go back in order to learn when, where, and how your problem began. You may be complaining about your uncaring relatives today, but that problem has built momentum with time, and now you can't stand it.

"Phenomenology also analyzes our presuppositions that is to say, when we have a sense that an idea has a preexisting implication or motive. Like, when you help one of your relatives, you think that you are doing it all for them, but in reality, you are also doing it for yourself.

This is where expectation plays a big role. Every time you advise or help, you are already anticipating certain outcomes because you are focusing your intentions on those certain outcomes, and when this outcome does not appear before your eyes, it is then that you feel betrayed."

"I think I get it," Charlie said thoughtfully.

"You see, it's like when you have a customer going to take a cross-country trip—a customer who you know is comfortably well off—and while his car is several years old, you see that he keeps it well maintained. But since this is an extended road trip, you tell him it would be wise to change the battery, the brakes, the shock absorbers, the timing belt before it snaps and even the crankshaft. You know that the car still has a lot of healthy miles before the belt would snap, and the brakes and shocks have lots of wear left, and nobody ever preventively replaces a crankshaft, but if you intimidate the ignorant client enough, you would get a big sale."

Affronted, Charlie bridled, "If I were that unethical, I'd lose my business in a New York minute?"

"Charlie, calm down," she soothed. "You and I both know in our hearts you could not and would not do such a thing. But, speaking completely theoretically, *if* a mechanic did this, you could expect a big pay day that you would not have otherwise. Am I right?"

Charlie quickly calculated the parts and labor in his head. "A big pay day," he said. "So, what?"

"Well, if we go back to the real reason for our conversation, we are talking about intention, and in the case of our last example, there was more reason to make money than to improve the life of the car. And those intentions are the idea before the idea that became the question for your client. In other words, when you suggest all the potential changes for the car before the trip, you know that some of those changes are not necessarily urgent, and if you do get to make all of *those 'important but not necessarily urgent changes,'* you will have an easy job, a happy client, and also extra money. Right?"

"Yes, but it's not right," Charlie nodded.

"It is the same when you help your relatives. You already have certain expectations, and because those expectations are not fulfilled, you find yourself gloomier than ever."

Finally, Charlie clicked in to Lucia's ideas. "Lucia, you know I hate it when you are right, but you are right."

"Bravo, Charlie, I also love your honesty. So now, tell me, my dear friend. What is the real reason you help your relatives? Do you want them to thank you? Do you want them to owe you something? Do you want them to praise you?" She raised her eyebrows. "What then is the real reason for your generous help?"

She saw Charlie mulling this question and continued, "Furthermore, if you are suffering *depression*, is it because you think that you will never know what exactly it is that you do for them? Ask yourself this question, 'How much am I willing to invest in my relatives?' I don't mean money. I mean, how much are you willing to invest of your own 'good will?' If you really would like your life to have any meaning, make sure you invest in your own good will."

Charlie sat pensively. Then, he slapped the top of his desk. "You know what, Lucia? I . . . I am going to think about all of this phenol-menolo . . . something. More than that, I think that I now understand the fact that when I help any one of my friends and relatives, I am not only helping them. I am also wanting something. This something is what I need to figure out before we have another philo-mechanic talk."

Manny tapped on the door. "Hey, boss, the battery on the charger is done. What do you want me to do with it?"

"Put it back in Lucia's car," Charlie said. Manny left without comment.

"What do I owe you?" Lucia asked, getting her credit card out.

"Consider it a straight trade," Charlie responded, "even if I did get the better side."

Sliding the card back in her wallet, Lucia said, "Charlie, you have been very kind, giving me an opportunity to throw my own philo-mechanics on your lap. By all means, let me know whenever you may be ready for another chat, and as you know, I will be here in a minute."

"One thing you can do for me right now," Charlie told her, "is let me have a great big hug." The two old friends embraced each other. "Thanks again, Lucia."

15

Pleasure or Happiness

W HEN NOT TEACHING or tending to her family, Lucia wrote a weekly column for the local newspaper. After her chat with Charlie, this is what she wrote:

My Dear Reader:

Pleasures, when well chosen, may offer the great gift of happiness, but often, we get caught with the thrills of the moment and fleeting pleasures, hoping to increase their intensity. Instead of promoting our pleasure on the road to happiness, we may find ourselves practicing hedonistic or self-indulgent tendencies and never getting close enough to genuine happiness.

How we transcend from pleasure to happiness is by putting into practice not only our sense perception but also our rational capacity, the way Aristotle the great Greek philosopher (384-322 BCE) recommended it in his lectures on ethics. He said that in order to move from pleasure to happiness, we must keep in mind "the real reason for our choices." When we feel a sort of internal calm, it is not because the weather is very nice but because we feel a kind of tranquility of spirit that produces internal peace, known as happiness. Happiness is not a direct feeling; happiness is always a by-product. Aristotle was a naturalist; thus everything was a chain of causes and effects. When the cause of our choices is motivated by "decent and noble conduct," the effect eventually guarantees the greatest personal benefit of experiencing genuine happiness.

Mother Teresa, during one of her visits to a very poor village in India, was offered the one and only available bed, but she declined, saying, "I don't need a bed, the ground is just fine." One of her followers replied, "But, dear Mother, you slept on the ground yesterday." To which Mother Teresa replied, "But that was yesterday."

Now, if I offer you my bed the way Mother Teresa was offered a bed, and you actually accept it, and I sleep on the floor, it is very important that I know why I have given up my bed. Was I after a pleasurable experience of having you thank me profusely? Was my ulterior motive to be nice so "you owe me one?"

And what is the importance of an ulterior motive? Even though you may wake up feeling great, thanks to me, my action would never be elevated to "a grand and noble cause," and Aristotle himself would never had given me any kudos for having given up my own bed.

We all know that we do different things for different motives. Some of us want to be famous, make money, or get public recognition, while others risk their lives for glory and good reputation. Fame, glory, riches, and good reputation may actually produce pleasure, but if that pleasure does not reach the category of a "grand and noble choice" of conduct because of jealousy, envy, greed, avarice, manipulation, extortion, social recognition, etc., the pleasure received is hardly worth mentioning and never part of any real happiness.

For some of us, it is hard to get away from "the old neighborhood" because we know that the benefits that we have received from our fame, glory, and good reputation are always in the hands of those that have made us famous or glorious. We know that the moment we move away from there, we will leave our fame and glory behind. Thus, these kinds of pleasures are only the means to a desirable end but never true happiness.

By the way, there are behaviors that are never good in themselves like thievery, murder, or adultery. One of my students once told me that after learning Aristotle's formula for perfect conduct, "the four rights," he wanted to convince me that true happiness is found when you are in the right place, at the right time, with the right woman, doing the right thing. But after three hours of arguing, I told my student to bring his arguments back to our next lecture because by midnight even the best of philosophies begin to fade away. But I never saw that student again. Do we wonder why?

Thus, the purpose of this philosophical news is to know the difference between pleasure and true happiness. When we contemplate a beautiful sunset by the beach that stretches all the way through endless miles in the perfect horizon of a lovely evening, we receive instant pleasure while we look at it, but if we close our eyes, keeping its radiant beauty in our mind, perhaps experiencing the most sublime "esthetic peak experience" ever, this knowledge of counting on the consistency of nature is what builds our trust as we wait with enthusiasm for the very next sunset. This is the consistency of "good and noble ethical choices" of the four rights that allows the exuberance of the momentary pleasure with the possibility to transcend into the eternal experience of happiness when we know better and we do what is right.

MARÍA ELENA PELLINEN

16

Philosophy or Grammar

S UNDAY. LUCIA SAT on her favorite bench beneath the shade of one of the tallest and broadest trees. She felt safe in this park; it was one of the few that showed little evidence of illicit activities, and to her knowledge, there had been only a few drug busts, and those had been two years in the past.

Lucia positioned herself on this bench, ready to give advice or talk out issues with anyone. Her first year teaching, she came to this bench on Sunday afternoons for quiet reading until her students discovered her there and came for extracurricular advice. Eventually, her prime purpose became giving advice, light tutoring, and philosophical discussion.

Sometimes while waiting for someone to sit, Lucia imagined her father at the opposite end of the bench. Today, the old gentleman, wise and relaxed, said to her, "Mira hija, don't ever say that you don't have a thing to do even when it feels like that is the case, and by all means, never waste your time. See the people in the park, the people passing by? Observe them. Analyze them. Draw a hypothesis of who they are. Shoes tell a lot about the person: fastidiousness, economic status. Observe their body posture and how they walk. Are they looking up with an air of pride and self-sufficiency or looking down, dragging their feet? What about their faces? Do you see a lot of wrinkles? Are they well earned, or are they prematurely chosen? Often people who develop wrinkles between their eyes are people that are constantly frustrated and upset. You must know, my dear daughter, that if you relax the muscles of your face, you will not wrinkle prematurely, and if you wear a smile more often than not, you will actually keep your youthful look for a lot of years. But above all, people will be happy to see your face if you keep a friendly expression, the same expression that adds beauty to anyone's face."

Lucia sat in reverie, remembering the *intentionality* of her father's thoughts while she watched people in the park. She blinked her eyes.

Her father's image had gone. Lucia opened up her copy of Sunday's *La Opinion*. She skimmed the editorial page and glanced up every so often, just in case one of her students, former students, or friends approached. She recognized a young man walking by. "Jason, good morning. How are you?"

The young man stopped abruptly. "Oh! Professor, I am sorry, I didn't see you. I have so many projects in my head that I was totally distracted." He smiled. "It's a good thing I'm walking on autopilot."

"So, how are you doing today?"

Jason squinted. "I'm not sure you want to go there."

Lucia patted the seat next to her. "It seems I am already there, my dear Jason. Honestly, do tell me. What is going on?"

"Well, I am very frustrated with my job," Jason said, sighing as he took the seat. "I haven't been promoted in a couple of years."

"You're an intelligent guy, and from what I remember of you in class, you're a hard worker. Why haven't you gotten a promotion?"

"I guess it's me. I don't put myself up because you have to take a comprehensive test to get interviewed for upper management. I'm afraid I won't pass," Jason admitted. "So I study and get copies of the practice tests, but by the time I feel I'm ready, the opportunity has already gone by, and I spend half of my lifetime wondering if I would have done well if I had taken the test. I'm in a vicious circle."

"My dear Jason, that 'if I had or if I had not had' is nothing but a grammatical device. Do you know that I am referring to the conditional perfect tense, using the word *had*, and I know what you mean when you say, "if I had." having no existence because you never followed through on the action."

"Wait a minute, Professor." Jason grimaced. "You think my issue with taking the test lies with my syntax? Interesting."

"How long have you worked for this company?"

"Four years."

"And you last got a promotion?"

"Two years ago."

"So for two years, you have lived with 'if I had.'" Lucia looked directly into Jason's eyes. "Honestly, what is the worst that would happen if you dare to take the test the next time that it comes around?"

"I could fail the test."

"And then, would you lose your job?"

"No, I would just stay where I have been for the last four years!"

Lucia smiled a reassuring smile. "So you would be no worse off than you are now, and you would possibly be quite a bit better. I recommend you need to dare to take the test, and one of those Saturdays when I speak at Kat's Café, come to visit me. Will you do that?"

"I'm still anxious about it, but I will. And, I will tell you how I did regardless," Jason promised.

"Listen Jason, when you see your frustration as a problem instead as a dead end, you will discover new energy because *problems always have solutions*."

A couple of weeks went by, and on a Saturday evening, Lucia strode into Kat's Café. Jason waited next to the baked goods display. He grinned from ear to ear.

"You passed!" Lucia exclaimed.

"I passed, and I aced the interview, and now I have a brand-new position that pays nearly twice than what I earned before!" Jason beamed. "My only regret is if I had taken that test at two years ago, I would have had a lot more money in the bank."

Lucia embraced him. "I am very, very proud of you," she said. "Now, my dear Jason, I want to explain to you again the same grammatical theory that we talked briefly about in the park. Since all our friends are here waiting for me to speak, I am going to include everyone in the conversation that I would have had just with you, and I hope you agree with me."

Jason gestured "be my guest" and took a seat with the others. His smile and face beamed brightly.

"*Buenas noches*," Lucia said. "And thank you for your presence. Today, I am going to tell you how unnecessary and useless and sometimes even dangerous it is to speak using the perfect conditional tense. In other words, any verb preceded by 'if I had or if I had not,' because those useless words actually carry a lot more force than you may think.

"Let's imagine a family scene where the whole family is sitting to have dinner, when all of a sudden one of the kids says, 'Mom, may I have some milk?' 'Sure dear, no problem,' says the mom. She opens the refrigerator to find out there is no more milk. She says, 'Oh, dear, I am sorry there is no more milk.' She has hardly finished saying that when her husband replies, 'You know dear, if you had called me before I left my office, I would have picked up milk on my way home.' At this point the father has redeemed himself of any wrongdoing, but the poor woman is definitely guilty as charged. What can she do at this point? Hopefully, she doesn't feel miserably guilty. If she could ask me, I would suggest that she says at least two things. One would be, 'Now you can drink water with ice or without it.' Or she can tell the husband that if the milk is so important, he can run to the store and buy it now. But we know that she would never say that because the husband already implied that she should have known better. And we know that if she had known better, she would have had milk in the refrigerator. *Please!* Don't ever allow that kind of talk, full of 'if you had or if you had not' to belittle someone!

"Then there is another case. A man stops by to visit a friend who is in the middle of his dinner. Shortly after the wife opens the door and invites her husband's friend to come in, she says, 'If I had known you were coming, I would have cooked another steak' to which her husband's friend replies, 'Thank you anyway.' But, thank you for what? The husband and wife did not offer a dinner, and now the guest thanks them for that 'potential steak' that never was."

"So, tells us, Professor, how can we get out of this grammatical trap?" said Lydia.

"When we recognize that the 'if I had or if I had not' is an idea never considered at the right time. This is the reason that when we speak using that grammatical form, there is always the unavoidable lamentation of a guilty thought or a string of 'I am sorry.' But saying, 'if I had or if I had not' cannot solve the problem. When we depend on one of those 'if I had or if I had not' statements, our behavior is more neurotic than healthy. After all, being human is never a perfect condition."

"So, Professor what should we say instead?"

"Let's put this way: if a man came to my office and said to me, 'You know, Professor, I have been married for twenty miserable years, but if I had not met that woman, I wouldn't be talking to you.' That very moment, I would say to myself, 'This man has to come to my office for a lot of sessions until he can recognize that he has in his hands the power to act or to choose. The only way to rescue one's mental health when we fall in the trap of the 'if I had or if I had not' is by exchanging it for the preterit, saying, 'I did it or I did not.' The preterit is the very second tense, the simple past, what you did. But that poor man would have to travel through seventeen grammatical tenses."

"What do you mean seventeen tenses, professor?"

"Well, allow me to write them down for you. The grammatical chart is divided by the simple and perfect conjugations, and this is the way it goes." Lucia pulled out the little whiteboard she brought for such occasions, and began writing and talking at once, listing verb tenses from the present to the past, on passed imperative, until with the seventeenth she arrived at "'I might have done.' Or 'if I had or I had not.'"

"Thus," she said, "when we learn to pay for the consequences of our poor choices by saying, 'I did it or I didn't,' we will be using all the force of our liberty and free will."

Jason piped up, "Professor, may I reinforce your concept?" He addressed the group. "A few weeks ago, Lucia explained the danger of 'ifs.' I followed her advice and went from avoiding taking a test because I thought *if* I failed, then *this* might happen to doing, to taking the test without considering the *if*. Now, I have a promotion, a raise that nearly doubles my income, and my life has changed 180 degrees."

The assembled group *oohed* and *aahed* over Jason's success. Many noted down Lucia's list of verb tenses. And Beatriz managed to give away all her delicious home-baked cookies before the session wrapped up and all went home. Thus, one more successful lecture at Kat's Café ended.

17

Agnostic or Believer

HEADING INTO THE Humanities Building on her way to teach her morning class, Lucia encountered Anthony, a grad student she had not seen since the previous semester, when he and his fiancé married. They exchanged pleasantries, and Lucia asked, "How is your lovely wife? I think I remember her name is Dawn, like the sunrise?"

Suddenly Anthony's energy evaporated. "Fine," he said without expression.

"As Abraham Lincoln said, 'You can fool some of the people some of the time' but not your former philosophy teacher," Lucia told him. "Is Dawn well? I hope she is not suffering something dire."

"Professor," Anthony said firmly, "you enjoy getting into peoples' lives and believe you can solve every little thing with a philosophical twist, but this is not a little thing. Dawn, she . . . she and I are not friendly and aren't living together. This morning she texted me that she wants a divorce."

"For heaven's sakes, Anthony," said Lucia, "explain to me what is happening to the two of you. You have been married not even three months. But, please come to my office. I am early today, and I have plenty of time to hear what is happening to the two of you."

"No time today. I'm teaching two intros to communication arts and a speech lab," Anthony explained.

"Then come to my house for dinner tomorrow, seven o'clock. Do you think Dawn would come? I can call and invite her."

Quickly, Anthony said, "No, don't call her. I have to talk to her today, especially after that text. I'll do my best to persuade her."

"See you tomorrow then," said Lucia optimistically.

Later that afternoon while Lucia held office hours, Anthony stopped by. "I spoke with Dawn. She says she will come to dinner tomorrow."

"Wonderful," Lucia answered. "I look forward to it."

Anthony hesitated. "Lucia, do you still have a little time to talk?" Lucia gestured for him to come in. He closed the door. "I thoroughly enjoyed your class, and I enjoyed the little talks we had after."

"Thank you. You were a very good student."

"Can I give you some background on Dawn and me?"

"Certainly, of course. But remember while you tell me, I am also interested in Dawn's point of view. So don't use your communication skills to persuade me that you are right and she is not."

"It's not that at all," said Anthony, smiling wanly. "I'm not thinking either of us is particularly in the right or in the wrong."

"You may think that," Lucia reassured, "but trust me. Every individual pleads his own case."

"This all started," Anthony began, "on a free afternoon before we moved in together. To look at us on that day, you would think you were looking at a romantic scene. But what we were really talking about was that neither one of us truly believe in the eternal and romantic love. Dawn said love is just an excuse to stop being alone. I agreed that was a strong argument, and we both agreed that people who swear they are so totally in love that they must marry are deluding themselves. I remember Dawn saying, 'Words are only words—that is what couples say to each other so they can justify living together. Clearly they are enamored, but the truth is they don't want to live separately.' I said something about the true reason for choosing to live together is purely for comfort, to which Dawn said, then why are we paying so much to live apart? If we live together, we cut our expenses radically. She said, each of us pay rent, electricity, water, and gas, and when one cooks for one person, it seems to consume more in food because there are always leftovers that are saved forever until they finally go into the garbage. She was right, you know. So we moved in together, shared expenses, shared sex, you know.

"Of course, families got involved. When are you getting married? When will I get grandchildren? When will you make it legal? All the living up to society's expectations stuff. So, Lucia, when we came here for me to complete my doctorate, we decided to make a show for the families and get married. And, we said we will just keep our secret of knowing that love does not exist, get married for the sake of our mutual economic benefit. You know: joint tax returns."

Lucia held her tongue. She wanted to unload her theory on selfishness. But it sounded like the woman could be just as culpable. Better to save her ammo for when she had both in her presence. She thought, *Can you imagine, what a beautiful moment it could have been if these two embraced Plato's Archetype of Love and moved this friendship from a sublime moment to the eternal? But how could they when they both were agnostic about love? How long could these two continue with their superb friendship, keep it at the level of a business enterprise?*

After Anthony left, Lucia pondered their situation. Both were highly intelligent: Dawn was an attorney, and Anthony was completing his PhD in communication—his second after a doctorate in architectural building design. Lucia soon concluded that the problems that arose between Anthony and Dawn were due to their stated belief that they were *agnostics of love*. She knew that generally we reserve the term agnostic for those who, while not atheist, do not have a firm belief in God because they don't see him, they don't feel him, and they do not understand his eternal existence. But agnosticism does not exclusively apply to a belief in a supreme being. She considered how philosophy treats belief or faith as something eternal and present, never has to be defended, clarified, or interpreted because it is always valid. Lucia's problem was how to convert an *agnostic* to a *believer*.

Dawn and Anthony arrived at Lucia's a few minutes ahead of seven, bearing flowers and a bottle of wine and looking for all the world like a happy, newlywed couple. Lucia realized she should have filled Gary in because the first thing he asked when they sat down for dinner was about their honeymoon.

Anthony said, "Dawn's aunt and uncle gave us an all-expense-paid honeymoon at a beautiful resort in Puerto Vallarta, the Mayan Palace. We had a blast fooling everybody."

"Fooling everybody about what?" Gary asked.

Lucia told Gary to put the plates in the oven on warm. Then she said sternly, "You two: come into my office now."

"So, instead of trying to find the archetype of genuine love, you enjoyed the idea of 'fooling' everyone more than anything else," Lucia said. "Then what?"

Dawn looked at Anthony like he had led her into a trap. Nonetheless, she blithely explained, "From there, we continued sharing everyday expenses, the household tasks of cooking, and so forth. But somehow, now that we were legally obligated to be connected, we kind of went to our own corners. Is that your sense?" she asked Anthony.

He nodded. "Dawn got depressed, and I got short tempered, and neither one of us wanted to talk."

Tapping her fingers on her desk, Lucia announced, "Now I'm going to talk. Your agnosticism for love, or the lack of belief in it, is very obvious. It is as if a psychic virus grew in your house and contaminated everyone and everything. In only a few months, your edifice of the 'love economy theory' was collapsing. Tell me: when you spoke to each other, was there no longer any respect between you? Using different words, you both would say the same thing: you are only taking advantage, and I no longer matter to you. Am I right?" Both Anthony and Dawn nodded. "And let me speculate," Lucia went on, "one of you told the other, 'I can't stand you any longer.' Then the other responded, 'I can't stand you either.' Then both of you told the other to get the hell out my house. Am I right?"

"Pretty much," Dawn said, impressed with Lucia's perceptions.

"Okay. Now listen, you two. Don't think what you want to say back to me. Just listen." Lucia spoke sternly as a headmaster. "I will bet you that, because of all this, you have not opened all your wedding gifts." Dawn's jaw dropped. This woman knew them as intimately as they knew themselves. Lucia continued, "You two married thinking that it was not worth doing it for love because, according to both of you, love does not exist. And I sincerely doubt your poor souls have the capacity to fall in love because each of you is more narcissistic than compassionate." She shook her head sadly. "It is such a shame that you thought you did not need to have love for each other to enter into marriage. And now, the same lack of love is the reason you are near divorce. I tell you, it is obvious to me that your economic theory is now your mutual bankruptcy. And, you know the biggest shame is that while taking your theory to its extreme, you both burned your own capital of *good will*, the same *good will* that had carried your friendship for so many years in the past.

"Let me explain," said Lucia, "how complicated love is. Even the old Greeks created for themselves three gods of love because one could not take care of it all. They divided it into Agape, Philia, and Eros. Agape is the god who maintains the intellectual relationship between two people. Philia represents the healthy love toward a friend, and Eros takes care of the sensual love.

"It is obvious that you two are completely out of tune and far away from all three of these gods. *Agnosticism* and the entertainment of the grand lie is now your biggest self-deception. Suffering deception occurs when one has been deceived, and that means you both suffer from a self-imposed lie. That lie moved both of you toward an emotional failure. Agape is no longer your intellectual guiding light. Philia lost the common trust you had, and Eros tired of the mechanical and meaningless practice of your physical love, where you never found within each other any loving spiritual satisfaction. Consider what José Ortega y Gasset, the mid-twentieth-century Spanish thinker, said: 'Love is the togetherness of two solitudes that know how to share the same space.' Or as my adorable mother would say, 'Love is like having two well-tuned pianos playing the same melody at the same time," said Lucia.

"Now if you want to recover the friendship you already had for so many years, you need to begin, first of all, putting into practice mutual *respect* because *respect* is always above *love*." Lucia stopped. She looked at both of them, clear eyed, and awaited their responses.

For a long moment, both stared straight ahead, then looked down into their laps. Then Anthony reached over and took Dawn's hand. They interlaced fingers. He said, "That I want to be apart from you is a lie. I want to give it a try—staying married and staying together—really staying together."

Dawn said, "I miss my best friend very much." Spontaneously and without self-conscious thought, they kissed passionately, not considering Lucia's presence. They finally parted. Lucia said, "Very well, I believe that tonight you have recovered the best part of your friendship, the part that you almost lost when that crazy idea of putting your economic theory of love into practice nearly killed everything the two of you had ever had. Shall we return to the table?"

"Yes," Dawn answered for both.

"Gary!" Lucia called. "*Mijo*, please bring the plates from the oven!"

Distantly, they heard Gary say, "Thank goodness! I'm hungry as a bear!"

Getting up, they returned to the dining room. Gary came in, holding two plates with oven mitts. "Hot plates! Hot plates!" he said and went for the other two.

"I am glad you came to talk to me *at the right time* and please continue to check in with me," Lucia told them. "I am always ready to help. Now, I'm ready for that wine."

18

Temporary or Permanent

"LUCIA, COME HERE, child," the elderly lady called. Eight-year-old Lucia bounded in to the house of her neighbor, a very nice Greek woman, whom she called Γιαγιά or Grandmother. Young Lucia looked into the dazzling dark eyes of Γιαγιά, the elderly lady's face framed by beautiful white hair. Γιαγιά asked, "Tell me Sweetheart, which do you think is more important—your friends or the sun?"

Without missing a beat, young Lucia replied, "Of course, the sun, Γιαγιά."

Γιαγιά responded, "So now tell me, how much will the sun be able to help you when you have problems at midnight?"

From that day on, Lucia was always willing to talk to anyone regardless of the hour. Her friends and students had her house phone number, just in case someone needed her at midnight.

Lucia listened to her phone messages. First up was Hilary. Lucia often marveled at the incredible aspects of memory. Hearing Hilary's voice brought to mind first meeting Hilary, then just twenty years of age, beautiful, kind, and intelligent. She recalled the happiness and lilt of Hilary's voice, the bounce in her step, and the brilliant highlights in her green eyes. When Lucia met her, Hilary had fallen in love with Pierre, fifteen years older.

Pierre was tall and handsome. He was charming, kind, and attentive to Hilary. He easily captured Hilary's heart. He had a son, Joachim, and he owned two quite successful businesses. He had an easy way about him and entertained Hilary with quips and jokes. She laughed more than she remembered laughing. The little boy was equally charming.

Soon, Hilary moved in. Joachim's mother took this opportunity to take custody of her son. Neither Hilary nor Pierre minded that too much because it gave them the house to themselves. Pierre gave her use of a car, gave her a budget to decorate the house, and encouraged her to hire a maid to take care of house cleaning. He presented her a lovely, white Persian cat. Hilary suggested they marry. Pierre told her, "When the time is right."

Two years passed. Pierre's two businesses took more and more of his time. Hilary sat at home, hoping and praying for just a weekend with Pierre, just a single day, just an evening, just an hour. Pierre's business occupied him more and more, taking him out of town, out of the country, accompanied by his loyal secretary.

Hilary found out about the affair. Heartbroken, she packed her suitcase, took her cat, and went back to the loving home and hearth of her parent's house. She was sure she would never fall in love again.

On the other side of the city, there was a young man named Philip. His wife deemed Philip useless. Five years and no children. What kind of a man was he? Philip's wife left him for another man. Philip rented a bungalow and furnished it with a bed, a leather recliner, and a fifty-inch flat screen TV. He put on weight. His friends teased him. He resolved to change himself and joined a gym.

One day, early in the morning, Philip noticed a beautiful young woman with dazzling green eyes. He gathered his courage and spoke to her. Hilary liked him too.

The beginning proved rocky. They kept each other at a distance. Neither wanted to open themselves to the potential of getting hurt again. Still, they encountered each other at friends' houses, the theater, and cafés, until one day, they felt they had fallen in love. They thought themselves lucky to have found such a compatible, empathic soul mate, and they decided to live together.

Very soon afterwards, Hilary told Philip she was pregnant. Stunned, Philip asked, "Who is the father?"

"You are, of course. There is no one else," Hilary responded, equally stunned.

"But I am sterile," Philip insisted. "Yolanda and I tried and tried, and then when she remarried, she immediately got pregnant, so it wasn't her." Doubt, fear, worry, jealousy, and anxiety began to fill him.

She touched his cheek lovingly. "My dearest," she said softly, "you are our baby's father. Maybe, somehow, your body knew that before was the wrong time, and now is the right time."

Philip took Hilary in his arms and swung her around in delight.

Hilary and Philip married, surrounded by their happy friends and ecstatic families. They had everything—love, understanding, and a baby on the way. Their families threw a big, joyous wedding with food, music, and dancing long into the night. Seven months later, an angelic, beautiful baby girl entered this world. They named her Joy, the same feeling they had about her birth.

Bringing up a child proved costly. Both took better-paying jobs, and with those jobs came long hours of work. At the gym where they met, Hilary became an aerobics instructor and then assistant manager. Philip received promotions from his sales rep job to district manager and then division manager. The new incomes allowed them to buy a big, new house with a good-sized garden where Joy could play. Hilary's mother moved in to the basement apartment to take care of their little Joy.

By the time of Joy's third birthday, Philip's division manager job occupied his time nearly eighty hours each week. Hilary taught classes at the gym eight hours every day Monday through Saturday and often stayed late helping her manager with the daily accounts. They barely saw each other, or Joy.

The phone message was short but to the point. When it was done, Lucia sighed. She was not a bit surprised to hear Hilary reaching out. She phoned back and invited Hilary to bring Philip to come and talk to her.

"He won't come," Hilary said, sounding quite defeated. "He doesn't have the time."

"Give me his number," Lucia said. She phoned Philip on his mobile. Philip agreed to come and talk. It was nearly impossible to say no to Lucia.

Thursday evening at seven, Hilary and Philip arrived together at Lucia's front door. The distance between them could not have been larger. Lucia escorted them to her front parlor and offered them tea. They greeted Lucia perfunctorily and took seats at opposite ends of the sofa; their bodies twisted away from each other.

Lucia began in earnest, peppering the two with questions, "Didn't you two share your mutual stories? Didn't you share with each other how much each of you had suffered? Didn't you take the time to be sure that you were doing what you both wanted?"

Philip sat and studied his own hands. Hilary respond, "Yes, Lucia, we did all of that, but . . ." and launched into a tedious recap of their situation.

Lucia thought, *Could it be that these two immature people used each other? She had her baggage full of bitter deceptions and so did he. The two of them suffered the same deceptions from former lovers, and they both felt the pain of abandonment. Could it be that they became mutual handkerchiefs? When all of their painful tears have dried and the stories have become old and boring, are the two of them still in love?*

It was acutely obvious to Lucia that the pair took advantage of each other as one takes advantage of an advisor, a priest, or a good friend, seeking comfort and validation. *If they had only been honest with me at the beginning,* Lucia thought, *I would have advised them that marrying a wounded person most often leads to a sad end. The worst of it is, if one or the other finds someone to listen to his or her new tale of woe, another tragic cycle starts.*

Suddenly Hilary said, "Are you hearing me? You seem somewhere else."

"Yes, Hilary, I understand you perfectly well," Lucia said. "Let's see if I can parse this. What happened between the two of you is that both of you were in the position of being each other's *transitional* lover. Sometimes this is called a rebound relationship, and it is usually temporary because you are not in a healthy state of mind, but you reach out to an opportune person for momentary comfort. The fourth-century philosopher St. Augustine would not have called it *transitional.* He would have called it *transgression* or what I call 'walking backwards.'"

"So you're saying we should never have married," Philip asked dourly, with a sidewise glance toward Hilary.

"Listen closely, guys," Lucia replied. "We must learn to be able to take the temperature of personal sincerity. St. Augustine himself said, "Do not look outward, look back into yourself; the truth dwells in the inner person." The *transgression* you committed is looking for someone to blame. This is what Adam did in Paradise when he accepted the fruit from Eve, knowing perfectly well what that meant. When you told each other your stories, both of you were competing to see who had suffered the most, which caused to pity each other. And that pity ultimately resulted in each of you losing respect for the other. My advice to you is stop talking about the past because you already have a daughter in the present. Both of you have to understand that the union of marriage is not something temporary but permanent. Both of you have constructed a house with a weak foundation. You have an adorable daughter for whom both of you need to reinforce your marriage and move forward. So, go home, return to your child, and return to her the joy for which she was named. When you got married, you signed a contract promising mutual

MARÍA ELENA PELLINEN

loyalty. Go home and put it in practice. Both of you are very young. And do not forget that life is long and benevolent."

Philip set his teacup down before him on the table. He stood, smoothed the wrinkles down the front of his pants, and said, "You're finished? That's that then."

"I hope you will consider what I said," Lucia added hopefully. Philip gave her a perfunctory nod.

"We will have a long conversation about this," Hilary stated.

"Yes. We transgressors will have a conversation," Philip said.

"Philip . . .," Lucia said, touching his sleeve. "I said what I said because I care for both of you. I urge you to make the effort, for your daughter, for Hilary, and for yourself."

"We will," Hilary interjected. "Thank you very much, and we promise."

Philip looked at Hilary with warmth for the first time during their visit. "Yes," he echoed. "We promise."

"You don't have to promise me," Lucia said. "Promise yourselves."

19

Philosophy or Biology?

A NOTHER THIRD SATURDAY, another evening at Kat's Café. Elena Rodriguez, a current Philosophy 102 student, brought her mother to the podium. "Professor Lucia, this is my mom. She's Lucia too but in English."

Lucia smiled warmly, offered her hand, and said, "Welcome Lucy. I'm Lucy, too, but in Spanish." The two women shook hands, spoke briefly, and Lucia began the evening lecture.

"*Buenas noches*, all. It is such a pleasure to see all of our returning friends and welcome new friends. We have an open discussion, conducted as a Socratic dialogue, which means while I guide the conversation, you should feel free to question and comment—in an orderly manner, of course. Now, we will share *magnanimous time*."

"I have a question." A newcomer, a teenager wearing a faded T-shirt raised his hand.

"Your name, sir?"

"David. What does that mean? *Magnanimous time*?"

"Thank you for opening the dialogue, David. And thank you for asking me to explain an unfamiliar term. My first language is philosophy, right, gang?" Lucia quipped, and the regulars laughed with appreciation. "So if I use a word you don't know, let's stop right there so I can define the meaning. My goal in speaking is not to enjoy the sound of my own voice and brilliance"—more chuckles from the regulars—"but to communicate clearly. What is more important to me is not what I say but how do you hear me, so that all of us are on the same page and committed to the discussion." She looked to David to see if he understood. He did and nodded to show he got it. "Now, *magnanimous time* means, according to Aristotle, that we are doing *the right thing at the right time in the right place for the right reason*. Imagine that these four *rights* make a perfect square with us in the center. That gives us the opportunity to have a *magnanimous time*."

"We learned that in class," Elena whispered to her mother.

A rather unhappy-looking woman in the second row got up to leave.

"Are you okay?" Lucia asked. "Do you need something?"

"I just remembered something," the woman said uncomfortably. "Sorry."

"Is it something we can help you with?" Lucia asked.

"I, um, my aunt is in the hospital. I have to go see her before visiting hours are over," she told Lucia.

"Good one," sniped Sam, an opinionated regular. "Are you sure you don't have to see a man about a dog? Or have to return a book to the library? Or forgot you had a dental appointment?"

"Sam," Lucia gently admonished, "that is hardly magnanimous of you." She spoke gently to the newcomer. "I understand. Go to see your aunt with our blessings. Then you will be doing *the right thing at the right time at the right place for the right reason.* Your magnanimous time square will be complete." The woman, still looking unhappy, quickly left. "Be nice, Sam," Lucia cautioned.

"Now, back to Aristotle. Did you know that Aristotle, besides being interested in philosophy, also had interests in biology, anatomy, physics, and pathology?"

Elena's mother, Lucy, brightened. "I didn't know Aristotle liked pathology. They don't say that on the TV shows I watch about what happens with medical examiners in the morgue."

"Absolutely," Lucia concurred, "And thank you for bringing up morgues. Aristotle accompanied his father, the physician Nicomachus, to observe him analyzing the bones, organs, and muscles of the deceased. The father and son made drawings of the dissected corpses—quite detailed and accurate. Today I want to talk to you about the relationship that Aristotle found between philosophy and biology.

"Aristotle said that 'man is a rational animal by nature' and found what we have in common with the vegetable kingdom and the animal kingdom and the rational kingdom. Aristotle said, like the plants, we require the *nutrients* of the soil, the water and the sun. I personally find it interesting that there are people who only worry about their intake of *nutrients* in relation to the way they look, which makes vanity their favorite sin. Like me." Lucia laughed good and loud.

Sam chimed in. "Aside from yourself, could you give us an example?"

"You've heard the term *narcissist*? It comes from the Greek myth about the young man Narcissus who fell in love with his own reflection. These narcissists are always trying to preserve their youthful look. Think about Janewood actors and actresses, or models who are concerned almost solely with their physical appearance.

Lucia asked, "Have you ever known someone, or maybe you have this ability, to *perceive* when something is not quite right or when something is about to occur? Like when dogs or horses are aware of an impending earthquake? This ability is popularly known as animal perception."

"I know," Elena added excitedly. "When I was five, me and my grandma and her dog Wyatt were at a chalet when Mom and Dad and my big brother went out on the ski trails. Grandma took us on a walk because it was nice and sunny, and we didn't see the big clouds rolling in. They came down so low that we got fogged in, and Grandma didn't know where we were or how to get back to the chalet. I remember she sat down on a rock and said to me, 'Sweetheart, I need you to be brave.' Then Wyatt came over and stood up on her knees and tried to lick her face. He started up the trail and turned around like he was saying, 'Follow me.' He did that a couple of times until Grandma said she thought Wyatt was taking us home. So we followed him, and he led us straight to the chalet. It's like Wyatt knew we were lost and knew exactly what we needed. Would you call that animal perception?"

"Yes, I would," Lucia exclaimed. "That was a wonderful example, Elena. Your experience with your grandmother and her dog speaks highly of what we call animal perception, and you will find this clearly defined by Aristotle.

"Now, let me tell you a story of why we should include our animal perception in our decision-making process. Oprah Winfrey on her show once presented the experience of a woman who had her arms full of grocery bags and could not be able to put the key in the front door lock of her house. At that moment, a man who had been walking by presented himself as a Good Samaritan and offered to open the door for her. She said that her first reaction was to say no, but she felt embarrassed. After all, the man wanted to do a nice thing for her. So, she said yes and gave him the key. He opened the door, she stepped inside, then he followed her in, locked the door, and raped her." The group responded with murmurs of disgust.

"That is horrible," said Elena's mom, Lucy.

"There are times we are better off reacting immediately to the messages we receive from our perceptions," Lucia added sadly. "When the woman spoke to the police, she told them repeatedly that she should have followed her first reaction because something was telling her not to accept help from that horrible man. The poor woman failed to apply her 'animal perception,' but she also forgot to use her *rational* part. So, my dear people," said Lucia, "are we learning how to use the best of Aristotle's philosophy during this discussion?"

Beatriz raised her hand. Immediately, all the regulars, Kat, and Lucia thought, *Cookies!* But Beatriz had something to say. "Now that you have so clearly explained animal perception, I believe I have learned that I—and all of us—to live a life of clarity must have *nutrition* in the broadest sense, *perception*, and *rationality* in constant balance, always guided by the master virtue that is *prudence,* in order to be able to put Aristotle's four *rights* into practice, and that is always doing *the right thing, in the right place, at the right time, and for the right reason.* Am I right, Lucia?" A few of the students sitting close to her applauded.

Sam commented, "I don't know what you're putting in those cookies, but I think I'd like some of that."

Lucia applauded too. "Thank you very much, Beatriz. You certainly have taken our chat to a wonderful end. I am very grateful to have had all of you here tonight, and I hope to see you again in three weeks, in the same place, at the same time, in the same Kat's Café. Quite magnanimous." Lucia was happy.

20

Depression or Deception

"**H**OW ABOUT I make us a pitcher of Sangria?" Lucia suggested to her guest, Betsy, escorting her to the back garden, lush with bougainvillea. Bees buzzed and birds chirped in the golden light of afternoon.

"Perhaps tea?" Betsy responded.

A few moments later, Lucia returned with tea and pastries. Lucia told Betsy, "Your mother was one of my best friends when you and your sister were very young. How is Poppy doing these days? Are you still close?"

"We talk at least once each week, sometimes more. Poppy hit a milestone birthday this year. She's forty. I passed that two years ago," said Betsy.

"Well, let me tell you, your mother—she was one of the most beautiful women of her day," said Lucia. "Tall and slender, beautiful dark hair with gorgeous green eyes. Sometimes even I envied her. She always seemed to get what she wanted—jewelry, fur coats, and I shouldn't say this, though you probably are aware, she came into her own and was never happier when she divorced your father."

"Don't feel bad about saying that, Lucia," Betsy commiserated. "Poppy and I felt better too. No more yelling between them. No more yelling at us for no reason. I mean, what kind of man carries on with two other married women when he has a wife and kids at home?"

"That's probably why the judge ruled for your mother: generous alimony for five years while she was finishing her college degree and child support and full custody of you two. She didn't have to work. I remember she would say to herself, "I am myself and my circumstances," exactly as she had learned when we studied the philosophy of Jose Ortega y Gasset," Lucia's expression turned sad. "But at the same time that your mother put in practice that philosophy, she also told herself,

I am going to live my life just the way the modern *hedonists* do it. *Pleasure for the sake of pleasure with a minimum amount of pain.*

"I know," Betsy said with regret.

"At that time, your mother told me your father advised her to return to the university and finish your degree. He reminded her the alimony only lasted five years, and then he would press to sell the house and divide the earnings on the property. Also within the same time, you and your sister should be at college or finishing your high school diplomas, so your mother needed to be self-sufficient or she wouldn't have my money. What a jerk." Lucia shook her head. "When your mother returned to college it seemed going back to school was a good and safe choice."

"Then it all went south," sighed Betsy. "Mother took the *hedonistic* lifestyle to heart. I know you remember the gin and tonics. Then she practically lived at the track betting on the horse races. When she wasn't there, she brought the jockeys home with her. Sometimes more than one at a time. Poppy and I ran wild too. Remember?"

"What I remember," Lucia said firmly, "was the day I picked you two up at school, and you stayed with me a month and a half. It was like you girls hadn't had a solid meal for weeks."

"We hadn't. Mother got so depressed and started buying cheesy romance novels and read all day. And the house...."

"I remember your poor home falling apart. I remember when I would go to check on your mother, the faucets would be leaking, the curtains falling off the rods, the dishes piled in the sink, and the grass about a foot high. And your mother would say, 'Lucia, dear friend, don't ask me any questions, just tell me about you.'

"Unfortunately, that meant that she did not want anyone to tell her what to do, not even me, one of her best friends. And before she knew, the famous five years had gone by, and the house got sold. Because the house was in such terrible shape, neither your mom nor your dad made any money from the sale. Shortly after, the two of you went on your own way, and your mom went to live with her last jockey who was drinking as much as your poor mother."

A pall fell over the room. The two ladies stirred and sipped their tea. Betsy stared out the front window; Lucia lightly cleared her throat. She moved a throw pillow from one side of the sofa to the other.

Poor Alice, Lucia thought, *in less than five years she lost her beauty, her personality, and her social position. All she did every day was drown herself in alcohol.* Lucia remembered Alice getting so lost in her alcoholic depression that her elderly mother came from the other side of the country to rescue her from her miserable existence. *What happened to Alice?* Lucia wondered. *What did the hedonistic life full of pleasure do for her?*

Betsy sipped the last of her tea and set the cup in front of her. "I really think my mother lost the awareness of the thin line between pain and pleasure," she said, sighing. "She drowned herself in alcohol."

"Do you mind if I speak candidly? Philosophically but candidly? I suppose that's my crutch," Lucia said.

Betsy nodded earnestly. Lucia recognized the longing, the yearning in her face.

Lucia continued, "Some people think alcohol washes off the problems when, in reality, it only irrigates them. Your mother forgot that in order to establish one's happiness, it is necessary to select, very carefully, *the right pleasures with the right moral choice, putting always in practice self-control and temperance.*" Lucia went to a bookcase and picked out a book. She placed it in Betsy's hands. "This book," she said, *Plato's Republic*, your mother and I shared when you were young. We read it out loud back and forth to each other to help our understanding. Do you know the quotation *'When the best part of me surprises, the worst I am the captain of my soul'*?"

"I think I have heard something like it," Betsy noted, studying the leather binding carefully, admiringly.

"Would you like to have the book as a memento of something we shared?" Lucia asked.

"I couldn't," Betsy protested. "I couldn't take your copy."

"It's one of many. Trust me. Take it with my blessings,"

"Thank you," Betsy said softly. She dabbed at a tear.

"So, down to business," Lucia stated. "You came here because you want me to talk to your mother, do you not?" Sometimes, Lucia used bluntness as a tool to move conversations forward. "Depression hits when one has been deceived or lied to. And in your mother's case, she created her own deception. What we need to learn is that for the average healthy person, depression and deception are perfectly linked as a self-created condition. That is exactly what happened to your mom. So, what's the best way to get in touch with her?"

MARÍA ELENA PELLINEN

"She called me yesterday from the Spring Leaf Shelter. That's why I called you. I haven't been able to bring myself to go down there. I haven't even told Poppy." More tears flowed down Betsy's face.

Lucia took Betsy's hand. "You know what you have to do, don't you? Do you have room in your house? What does your husband say about this?"

"I think it would be okay. I mean, I haven't told Steve either, but he converted our garden shed to a guest house a couple of years ago, and it mostly sits empty."

"That's good," Lucia stated emphatically. "You go get it ready, and then you and me will go down and get your mother. Betsy, I lament tremendously not having been able to give her my help. She has been one of my best friends. Maybe now she will allow me to give her my help."

"Thank you, Lucia!" Betsy hugged her hard.

21

Love or Respect

LUCIA'S CELL PHONE rang. She quickly glimpsed the caller ID. She felt that was wrong, but she did it anyway. She felt one should take whatever the world brought as a gift, and knowing what—or who—was calling was, in a way, cheating that gift, like sneaking peeks at your presents before Christmas day. Still, it made her happy to know her friend and colleague Bertrand, a professor in the chemistry department, was calling.

"Hello, Bertrand! What can I do for you today?" she asked.

"Lucia, I need a letter."

"Of course. To whom, about what, and when do you need it?"

"Oh, my," Bertrand said nervously, but that was perfectly normal. Bertrand always seemed a bit nervous, perhaps because of one too many explosions in the lab. "Frederick and Laila are going to a seminar this weekend. It's for young people about to be married for the first time."

"Congratulations. Why did you wait so long to tell me, or did they just decide to do this?" Lucia asked. "Do I know this Laila?"

Bertrand stuttered for a good minute or so. Lucia held her tongue. Her friendship with Bertrand taught her it was best for him to do this without help. She wondered if the cause was physical or mental. Finally, he said, "The people at the seminar suggested the participants ask relatives and friends write them a letter expressing all their sincere sentiments about their relationship and intent to get married. Laila is the civil engineering student I introduced you to at last April's mixer."

"The Hawaiian girl? The one who's been around since Frederick went to high school? Of course, I'll write it. Bertrand, I am honored. I will drop the letter by your office this afternoon."

"Oh my," Bertrand said as he hung up.

Lucia immediately sat down and wrote:

My dear Frederick,

I have a question for you. Do you know how to bring the past all the way to the present? Well, according to St. Augustine of Argelia, we can bring the past to the present, thanks to our memory.

I know, Frederick, those years ago you noticed a very lovely young lady who wore a constant smile, and then you noticed that, by chance, she was in every one of your classes. You said hello, shared class notes in common, and schedules, and both of you continued being classmates for a while. After all, both of you were still very young.

What was very enchanting to you was that she always kept track of all the details of your conversations, and she would also ask how things were with you.

That became for you a true revelation of sincerity and affection, to the point that you realized that you mattered to her because she was demonstrating that she cared for you.

Then one lovely afternoon you waited for the perfect time, with all the energy that comes from the inner part of the soul, to ask her if she wanted to be your sweet heart.

How wonderful! Your wish had become a reality, and now dating had begun. Together, both of you finished high school, and both of you continued studying at the university, and that romance between you kept blooming like the most wonderful tree, so tall and so healthy. I imagine you thinking that the time was right to say to that beautiful girl, "My love, I have everything, but you. Would you marry me?"

And I imagine bells rang in her heart, and with the happiest and most explosive shout she said *yes*!

Without a doubt, both of you cared for each other, knew each other, and now were in love, but above the tallest mountains full of love between both of you, there was a great deal not only of love but also of respect, the necessary ingredient for the perfect eternal friendship.

And today, both of you are yet to sign the legal contract that makes you husband and wife. Like the philosopher Jose Ortega y Gasset would say, both of you are already married because for you "love is the togetherness of two solitudes," or as I have mentioned before in my mother's own words, "Love for the two of you is like the sound produced by two pianos that carry the same melody."

Lucia con amor!

MARÍA ELENA PELLINEN

22

Lady Fortune and Lady Reason

DISTRACTED MOMENTARILY BY the passersby in the afternoon sunlight, Lucia turned her attention back to the slew of unread e-mails on her iPad. *How am I ever expected to keep up with everything?* she wondered. *Classes, students, the ad hoc seminars at Kat's—the house!* Thankfully Gary had no qualms stepping in and keeping the house running. Thank goodness Gary was forward thinking and not mired in unworkable traditionalism. But then if he was, he would never have gotten involved with her, Lucia thought, way back then. Glancing down at the screen, six down on the list, Lucia saw an e-mail from her friend Sandy in Kuwait.

"Good afternoon, Professor."

Now Lucia looked up to see Cesar, a student who was in classes last spring. He had that look, the look that says, "May I sit down? I have something urgent to discuss." Lucia gestured to the chair opposite her in the coffee bar. "Would you like to join me, Cesar? Can I buy you a coffee?"

Taking the seat, Cesar held his very large coffee cup for Lucia to see. "They told me I could find you here. They said you come almost every day around this time."

"I see. So, what can I help you with and who are 'they'?"

"You know," Cesar answered, "them. Everybody that knows you."

"Wow. That's a lot." Lucia folded her hands on the table and adopted a serious demeanor. "Tell me what's on your mind."

"Do you remember Jeff?"

"Jeff? You're going to have to help me out with more than that. I have known many Jeffs."

"Jeff Kaminski. He was in the class I was last spring? Kind of quiet? Sat on the row next to the hallway?"

Lucia remembered. "Of course. Jeff. I saw him shortly after his grandmother had died. He stopped by my office and told me she left him a good sum of money."

"Thirty-five thousand dollars," Cesar told her.

"My," Lucia said. "He wanted to talk but was running late to work, I think. He said he was going to use it toward college."

"Yeah, well, that didn't work. He bought himself a used Porsche."

"For heaven's sakes! His parents must be very upset."

"Yeah, and he drove it off the lot and took it up on Wild Canyon road and slammed into the rail at Hairpin Turn."

"Oh my god," Lucia exclaimed. "And Jeff? Was he terribly hurt?"

Cesar shook his head. "Lucky for Jeff the Porsche was new enough to have air bags. He got bruised up, but the car was totaled."

"Well, thank god for insurance," Lucia said.

"That's the problem," Cesar smirked. "Paid cash, drove it off the lot, never called All State."

"How do you like that? Bad luck, his grandmother dies. Good luck, he inherits money. Good luck, Jeff is fine. Bad luck, the car was not insured." Lucia sighed. "How long are people going to be throwing their fortunes the same way we throw a yoyo? Because when the yo-yo goes up is good luck, but when the yo-yo goes down is bad luck."

Cesar agreed. "If it weren't for bad luck, I'd have no luck at all."

"My philosophical advice is to stop using the celebrated phrase of 'good luck' unless we find ourselves playing cards at a casino, hoping to walk out of there millionaires as soon as we become lucky," Lucia stated. "Cesar, do you remember when I spoke about Boethius while we were trying to make sense out of Julie's accident?"

"Yeah. I think so. She was the one who landed in the tree?"

"As you may remember, Boethius was the fifth-century philosopher who wrote *The Consolation of Philosophy*. I very much recommend that you read this book. Once you do, you will never be the same.

"For Boethius, Lady Fortune represents the unstable human condition that we could have because one day, she is on your side but not the next, and we never know when she is on our side. Boethius recommends we befriend Lady Philosophy because this lady is always the same. She is consistent, and she never betrays you. Taking Jeff as an example, we recognize his problems began when he befriended Lady Fortune, simply following only his emotions and abandoning completely the sincere friendship of Lady Philosophy and therefore letting go of the application of his reason."

"The temptation to run away from Lady Reason may actually happen more often than not," Lucia continued, "because when we respond to emotions one way or another, we get an immediate reaction, and if the response is not what we hoped for, then we rescue ourselves with wishful thinking such as 'God only knows' or 'This is my fate' or a simple 'We'll see what happens . . .,' always hoping for some kind of miracle or sheer luck." She took both of Cesar's hands in hers. "Cesar, we must make the effort to stop thinking in terms of 'good luck.' We have to start using the aid of reason as our strongest ally, always walking in the same direction of the legal, moral, and ethical route.

"Do you know that the biggest danger exists when Lady Fortune is on our side? Because she is kind, amiable, nice, and friendly, but also ephemeral and volatile, and she can get lost in a split second. Her presence is so real that when we see her close to our relatives and friends, we develop envy and jealousy without truly knowing why that person is doing well. We even say things like "You are so lucky . . .""

"Some guys are so lucky. Not me," Cesar said with regret.

"Let's go back to Jeff and think philosophically. His grandmother died, and that was very sad. She leaves him money—that was an opportunity. But very soon, Jeff put himself in the hands of Lady Fortune and bought a car. Lady Fortune left him in the next curve, and he had an accident without insurance. Lucky Jeff was unharmed but now penniless. How do you think Jeff is doing now? Remember class and think philosophically, Cesar."

Cesar considered, thinking back. "He must be suffering a big deception!"

"You are absolutely right! Deception is the right analysis because he deceived himself when he spent the money buying a car instead of saving it for university the way his grandmother intended it," Lucia confirmed.

Cesar grinned. He felt proud he figured something out using philosophy. "That's good. That's good," he repeated, celebrating his accomplishment. "Professor, do you have time for another cup of coffee?"

Lucia stood, slapping the table lightly but definitively. "Well, if I leave my decision in the hands of Lady Fortune, I do and I would enjoy another cup of coffee with you. But if I choose Lady Reason as my number one advisor, I will tell you that I don't have any more time because I don't want to walk in late to my next commitment."

"Didn't you say in class, 'Stress is produced by the accumulative momentum of unfulfilled personal promises?'" Cesar asked.

"You're right," Lucia answered. "Therefore I better run. But tell me quickly. What about school? Are you coming back?"

"Don't worry, Professor. I am already registered for next semester."

"Good boy, Cesar. That sounds wonderful because there is nothing better than the good investment of the internal capital."

Lucia was on her way. Suddenly, she remembered the e-mail from her friend Sandy. She sat on a bench and pulled it up on her iPad. It read, "Arriving Flight 6188, 2:45 PM. Looking forward to seeing you and spending quality time! Sandy con amor!"

23

California or Kuwait

G ARY AWOKE TO bustling in the nearby bathroom. He blinked his eyes and put on glasses. The clock read 6:45. Gary climbed out of bed and stood in the bathroom door, admiring Lucia fussing with her hair. "Good morning," he said, "You're up early. What's up?"

"I told you two days ago. I'm picking up Sandy at the airport," she replied, mildly irritated.

"I think I would remember that." Gary returned and sat on the bed, wondering.

Lucia came into the bedroom concerned. "Maybe I didn't tell you. Or maybe I meant to and forgot. What else is bothering you?"

Gary did not look up. "I suppose she's staying here, whoever she is. That's how it works, isn't it?"

"I guess I've been so wrapped up in my excitement, I made the mistake of assuming we talked about this. I am sorry, *mi novio*." She kissed the top of his head, on his bald spot. "Sandy was one of my students during my first years teaching philosophy in college. We got back in touch with Facebook. I know this is another imposition, but I invited some of my old students—Sandy's generation from college—to come to dinner. And yes, she will visit us for three days in our guest room. But that's not all that's bothering you. What is it?" Lucia stroked his arm.

Gary hung his head low. He sighed and breathed deeply. "I'm forgetting things. I'm wondering . . . I'm thinking . . . Am I losing it, Lucia? I don't want to be like my father."

"You are not your father," Lucia asserted firmly. "And you're not forgetting. You can't forget what I don't tell you."

"Well," Gary said, getting to his feet. "I'll make up the guest room. How many for dinner this evening?"

"A table full."

"Would you like your grandmother's turkey mole?"

"That would be perfect, dear one."

"Let's see. I have to shop: chocolate, peanuts, and sesame seeds that go on the mole as the last ingredient. Your mom gave me the recipe, and I will never forget it because she was such a wonderful cook," said Gary.

Their children Laura, Ellen, Sam, and Alexandria joined them in the kitchen for breakfast. They were excited to know a visitor—a visitor from outside the country—would arrive today.

"Mommy," Ellen asked, "could you tell us about your friend?"

"Of course, I will. Sandy is an American girl who took several of my philosophy courses years ago. Shortly after she went off to graduate school, she fell in love with a young man from Kuwait. Do you know where Kuwait is located?"

The girls exchanged glances. They knew it was somewhere in the Middle East, and they remembered something about the Gulf War but knew nothing specific.

"Sorry, Mommy," Ellen admitted.

"Don't worry about it. This is why Socrates said, 'I only know that I do not know anything.' All of us have a lot to learn. Okay. Let's see."

"Wait," said Sam, "I will tell you all about it. Kuwait is located on a corner of the Arab Gulf. Toward the south it is bordered by Saudi Arabia. To the north there is the Republic of Iraq. Am I right, Dad?"

Gary said yes, and the girls nodded, too, remembering from the news of the war.

"When Sandy finished her degree," said Lucia, "she married the man from Kuwait, and they moved to that country. The young husband, you see, grew up in the Arab environment, and all his customs, music, religious rituals, and language were from Kuwait. If I am not mistaken, Sandy had grown up with very little religious influence. When she arrived in Kuwait, she began to familiarize herself with her husband's religion, and she discovered a lot of human values that were soothing to her. Then, after she learned Arabic, she converted to Islam and accepted Muhammad as the prophet. I haven't seen her since she married. But now, she comes to visit."

"That's exciting," Laura said. "And we'll get to meet her and talk to her?"

"Yes, you will," Lucia assured.

A few hours later at the International Terminal, Lucia observed Sandy making her way through Customs. Physically, she had changed little; her figure was still trim, and her face vibrant and youthful. Sandy dressed traditionally for the contemporary Muslim world, wearing a black silk top buttoned to the wrist, black silk pants gathered at the ankle, and a demure scarf covering her hair. Once she cleared Customs, Lucia caught her in a great big hug, and they joyfully embraced, erasing years of separation. They drove straight to Lucia's house, chattering all the way, mostly about where this student and that student had gotten, Lucia's casual seminars at Kat's Café, and the doings around the university. Entering her house, Lucia said, "Let me mix up a big pitcher of sangria!"

Sandy demurred. "Perhaps just tea?" she asked, lowering her eyes. In the kitchen, while the water boiled, Sandy removed her scarf.

"That's what I remember. Beautiful strawberry blonde hair," Lucia complimented.

Gary came through the back door carrying an armload of groceries. Sandy quickly covered her hair with her scarf, and Lucia introduced the two. They greeted each other warmly, and once Gary had the groceries in, he carried Sandy's luggage to the guest room.

Lucia asked, "What's with the scarf? Why did you put it back on when Gary came into the kitchen?"

"A married woman always has to cover her head when men are visiting the house," replied Sandy.

"Including your husband?" asked Lucia.

"No, that is the exception," Sandy responded.

Later in the day, Lucia noticed Sandy putting a little Persian rug on the floor in her room, kneeling and putting her head on the ground. Lucia asked, "I know this is part of the Islamic tradition, but I have to admit I know little about it. Do you mind explaining to me? I'm curious."

"First of all," said Sandy, "the rug must be placed in the direction of Mecca, the holy city of Muslims. Our prayers are in the form of a conversation in which one asks Allah to remove all the temptations and to give us strength against the evil that Satan places in front of us, such as the temptation to steal, take drugs, to get drunk, to lose self-control. We also ask forgiveness for our offenses. We also forgive our offenders, and we thank Allah for the well-being that is surrounding us, and this ritual we put into practice five times a day in order to continuously remind ourselves of the qualities and the good intentions of our religion. But actually to comprehend better how Islam works, all of us know a parable. Would you like to hear it?"

"Of course, I would love to hear it," said Lucia.

"The story explains the life of the ascetic—that is to say, austerity, sobriety, moderation, frugality, and piety. All of that represents the philosophical meaning of Islam."

"Keep going, all of this is extremely interesting," said Lucia.

"Okay," said Sandy. "The story goes as follows: One day a man woke up very early, nearly at dawn, in order to pray at the mosque—the church of the Muslims. That man, named Saad, washed himself, put on clean clothes, and left his house. Halfway to the mosque, he fell down and got all his clean clothes dirty. He returned to his house, cleaned up, changed his clothes, and left again for the mosque. But again poor Saad fell and got dirty! He returned to his house again, cleaned up, changed his clothes, and again left for the mosque. Then the whole thing happened a third time. By now, he hardly had any clean clothes to wear. But this time, he did not fall as he walked to the mosque. A man got close to him and gave him a lantern to light his way. Saad asked him, 'Who are you?'

"The man said, 'I saw you fall three times, and that is why I brought you this lamp.' Saad thanked him profusely, and both of the men walked toward the mosque. When they arrived at the door, Saad asked the man to go in with him to pray, and the man said no.

"'Why won't you come inside to pray?' asked Saad.

"And the man replied, 'I don't pray because I am Satan.' Saad couldn't believe that Satan helped him so much. 'Look,' said Satan. 'I saw you leave your house and head toward the mosque, and I was the one who made you fall. You got up, went back to your house, cleaned yourself up, and left again. When you did it for the second time, God forgave you for all your sins. The third time you went back to your house to change your clothing, God forgave your family for all the sins they committed. Then I became afraid,' said Satan. 'I realized that if I made you fall one more time, God would forgive you for all the sins of your community. Therefore, I decided to help you arrive safe and sound at the mosque.'

"The moral of the story," said Sandy, "is don't ever allow Satan to benefit himself from his actions and don't ever stop making your good intentions a reality because you never know what kind of benefit you may obtain from accepting suffering and pain when you are trying to do things that are good, decent, and honorable. That is to say, don't fall into the temptation of avarice, fame, glory, pleasure, arrogance, or the excesses of tyranny, despotism, or plain abuse because you believe you can increase your personal position. All of those supposed benefits never really belong to you. To the contrary, those are human weaknesses that impoverish the good, honest, and creative spirit."

"What a wonderful explanation," Lucia said. "I must make time to study the ways of Islam. I'm sorry to say the faith has suffered a bad reputation, thanks to the men who terrorize people all over the world. But I know their philosophy is far different from yours."

"Thank you. I knew you would understand. Sometimes I hear dread in my parents' voices when we speak. They would be much happier if we lived here, preferably next door to them!" Sandy laughed. "My husband and I remain in Kuwait to educate our children until they are of age so they know the difference between the Eastern and Western world. We want them to know that human *compassion* is part of the inheritance of the Eastern world in contrast to the *competitive* behavior of the life in the West."

"Completely understandable," said Lucia.

"Lucia," Sandy said urgently, "during your philosophy lectures, would you advise your students to read the Koran as part of your literature and try to understand its good and healthy intentions of love and universal peace in order to make sure they do not misinterpret the good people of Kuwait?"

Lucia took Sandy's hand and patted it. "Bless you, my dearest friend, for everything that I have learned this morning. When our friends and colleagues come to dinner and enjoy the wonderful mole that Gary is already preparing, I would love it if you would tell them the Muslim parable."

"For me," said Sandy, "it would be an honor to share such philosophy." She inhaled deeply the aromas of Gary's cooking that permeated the house. "I am almost drooling from the smell of that wonderful dinner Gary is preparing."

"Me too," said Lucia. "Me, too."

24

Peace or War

L UCIA'S FORMER STUDENTS, Sandy's classmates, came into the foyer as a jocular mob, greeting and hugging. "How did you manage to arrive at the same time?" Lucia asked.

Suzy laughed. "Everything is not a magical coincidence, Lucia. We met at the mall, and all eight of us came in Frank's SUV."

"Then that was good planning."

"Plus," Frank added, "we didn't want to take up your whole street parking or have some of us park blocks away."

"Especially me," Ben said. "Don't want to get stopped in your neighborhood for walking while black."

Directing the guests into the living room, Lucia said, "Gary's in the kitchen whipping up a wonderful supper."

From the kitchen, Gary called, "Hola!" and they all responded.

"These are homemade tortilla chips and guacamole," Lucia pointed out. "You know, yesterday the kids asked me about Kuwait, and when Sam described its geographical location, they immediately knew where it is due to the unfortunate association of the war. How sad is this? It is so typical of all human existence that even mythological gods would force their own citizens to fight against each other claiming the privilege of superiority."

"You got that right," Ben spoke. "Remember in the Old Testament, God challenged Abraham to prove he was his faithful and loyal servant by taking his son Isaac to the top of the mountain to sacrifice him? That is seriously messed up."

Glynis added, "Yeah, but when Isaac had his back turned and Abraham took his knife to stab him, God sent an angel to stop him and told him to sacrifice a sheep instead. So that was good. And maybe that is the reason I don't like lamb."

"Not so good for the sheep," Frank offered, and they laughed.

"And that's where the prayer, 'O Lamb of God who takes away the sins of the world, have mercy on us,' comes from," Gayle noted.

Lucia furrowed her eyebrows. "I think we need to refresh you on biblical literature, Gayle," Lucia said. "Which gives me a thought: sometime soon at one of our Kat's Café nights, we can talk about Kierkegaard's interpretation of this biblical passage."

"Supper's on!" Sam announced from the dining room.

Gathered around the table and enjoying Gary's dinner, they caught up with each other, all the wheres, whens, who got married, who had children—all the typical subjects long-separated friends talk about. Of course, in this house, the topic drifted to philosophy.

Glynis asked, "Hey, Lucia, do you remember your philosophy lecture when you talked about the concepts of war or peace from Plato's philosophical point of view?"

"Let me see," said Lucia. "I think I must have told you that during Plato's lifetime there were all kinds of human experiences, just like now—love and hate, forgiveness and vengeance, knowledge and ignorance, rich and poor, good and bad, but especially just and unjust. I remember telling you that Plato had plenty of available material for his *Republic,* where he described his utopia—a perfect society."

Immediately, the friends became students again, giving their rapt attention to Lucia.

She continued, "Socrates suggested that in order to develop a utopia, the first thing to do was to find the ideal location with a balance of the four seasons, as well as all the public institutions such as schools, libraries, docks for commerce, stores, restaurants, theaters, and stadiums—without forgetting the Oracle, to praise the gods. And of course, it had to have a hospital, not just for the ill and infirm, but because some of the citizens would always behave in excess and need medical care."

They all laughed again, just like they did the first time Lucia described this to them.

"Let's continue with the condition of the human element, the rulers, the craftsman, and the guardian class, which we know as the police or the army."

"I've always wondered, Lucia," Suzy stated, "why did Plato's ideal government need to have police and armies? Isn't that a contradiction to the ideal?"

Lucia nodded. "You are so right, Suzy. But if you think about it, the armed forces have been the power of the ruling classes throughout the centuries. And, Plato, as intelligent and creative as he was, did not know how to eliminate the need for armies and police in a society that was supposed to be perfect. Poor Plato, he did not know differently since during his own lifetime he experienced several different kinds of government: democracy, military regimes, and even timocracy or oligarchy, where power was derived from honor and wealth. He met a few tyrants and despots in his day, and don't forget his beloved friend Socrates was executed in Athens during the time of a democracy.

"I would say," added Lucia, "that Plato seems to have recycled ideas, thinking he had created an ideal perfect society that would stand as the model for the rest of humanity, the same ideal society that has remained inside of the philosophy books. But let's come forward to the twenty-first century and think for a moment. What is the level of our civilization? And how much progress have we made since Plato spoke of this utopia?"

The assembled friends looked mutely at each other.

Lucia became expansive. "Come on! We have landed on the moon, and we can communicate with anyone throughout the world in an instant. If we are capable of this, why can't we have original thoughts that no one has had before? Why do we have to be so dumb and think that our greatest strength is our armed forces? Why do we insist on changing the governments and customs of other countries when their own ways have worked for thousands of years? Why should they be like us? Is it because *we* do everything so well that we have been in unnecessary wars for the past ten years and we have no idea when or how they will end? What kind of political culture do underdeveloped countries have? I would say that we are in the same condition in which Plato lived. Don't you think that our government is at various times as democratic, oligarchic, and timocratic because we have laws and money and armed forces? How much have we changed if we only have increased the amount of things and gadgets in the world?

Now we have so many city lights and pollution that even on clear nights we have difficulty seeing the stars. In Plato's day, not only could they see the stars, they could also see Venus, Mars, Mercury, and the rings of Saturn. Those were indeed divine and clear nights!"

"All right, y'all," said Benjamin, "you know what happens next, right?" The assembled friends chuckled. Benjamin stood and did his best Lucia impression, hand on hip and his napkin on his head. "Let's make a philosophical reflection and ask ourselves, Have we improved at all? Are we the same or are we going from bad to worse? Let's not forget that now we can hardly see the stars!"

Lucia laughed. "So, it is going to depend on each one of us to clean our interior home, that is to say, our souls, as we improve our integrity by increasing our civic responsibility," she said. "We need to help each other instead of waiting to see which team loses and which team wins. Who can truly brag about peace and winning the war while others suffer the loss? Let's make our own contribution on an individual level, putting into practice goodness, honesty, love, beauty, justice, and friendship. Who knows, with a little bit of optimism, if we take this seriously, maybe someday, we will be able to see all the stars of heaven again."

"Here, here," Benjamin said softly, and the others repeated under their breaths.

Lucia raised her glass. "Let's toast to all the good intentions we have discussed during this night when we have gathered to welcome Sandy, who came all the way from Kuwait, demonstrating her heart full of love and good will!"

Gary carried in a serving dish with a beautiful flan covered in ripe strawberries. The gathered friends applauded. Benjamin offered a chair. "Sit down, man. Who do you think you are? The chef, the waiter, and the busboy? That looks too delicious."

Joining them, Gary took a big drink from his still full wine glass before cutting into the flan.

"Sandy, I am ready to stop talking and enjoy this lovely flan," said Lucia. Would you tell us all the Muslim parable you told me that we should all put in practice?"

25

Knowledge or Wisdom

HAIR BY RAMÓN occupied a narrow storefront on a gentrifying street just three blocks from Lucia's house. An empty corner store, formerly a family-owned pharmacy, stood deteriorating nearby. Lucia hoped that corner would soon be occupied and giving support to the other new businesses—a nail salon, an antiques boutique, and a cupcake bakery.

Ramon Sanchez came to the university from Puerto Rico and liked the town so much that he stayed even when he was unable to finish his college degree. He got an AA from the community college and a certification in barber and hairstyling skills and opened his own shop. He did good work, and Lucia gave him her patronage.

"Hello Ramon," Lucia announced. "Here I am and, as you see, with my hair plenty long. I thought that if I didn't come to see you, I was going to have to cut my own hair. But I always try to remember Plato's words, 'We must respect peoples' expertise, allowing everyone to excel to his or her own craft."

Ramon spun the chair around for Lucia. "Let's see what we can do about that unruly mop," he joked.

She watched in the mirror. Ramon assessed the condition of her hair, expertly pushing it this way and that. "You know, Ramon, you really have chosen the perfect profession because hair grows and grows. You have job security. Some come too early, some come too late, but little by little, they all come. I am one of those who are a little too late," Lucia said. "I have been very busy. I had guests at my house."

"Who came to visit you, Professor?" Ramon asked, beginning to comb out her hair.

"Remember Sandy? I think you were in that class with her," said Lucia.

"Sandy? I remember her. What's she up to?"

"Married and raising her children in Kuwait," Lucia told him.

"I don't understand why anybody would want to do that. All the war and terrorism over there." Ramon chose a pair of scissors and began the trim.

"Don't lump all countries and peoples together," Lucia cautioned. "They are all different."

Ramon focused on his job. Lucia quietly enjoyed the rhythmic *snip, snip, snip*. He paused to look her in the eyes in the mirror. "Professor, could you clarify something for me?"

"I'll do my best."

"Something bothers me," he said. "How is it possible that there are young people graduating from the best universities and at the same time they can be so corrupt. I don't know who to trust. Over the weekend, I rented a couple of old movies: *Wall Street* and *Crimes and Misdemeanors*."

"I like those too," said Lucia. "Especially *Crimes and Misdemeanors*. It especially brings up questions of morality and ethics."

Ramon resumed trimming. "Greed is good? You can get away with horrible crimes? I mean, they were good movies, but the people were so corrupt."

Lucia agreed. "It is because the characters were blessed with knowledge but not with wisdom."

"So what's the difference?" Ramon asked, looking at Lucia's face in the mirror while he trimmed.

"Ramon! Watch what you're doing! Don't get too distracted and cut my hair shorter than I like it," said Lucia.

"Don't worry," the hairdresser chuckled." I can guarantee you that I can listen to you and give you a Hollywood haircut at the same time."

"Okay, Ramon," Lucia began. "First, think for a moment about the poor little farmer who lives up in the mountains completely isolated from technology and communications. As a matter of fact, think of him as someone who never had the opportunity to learn to read. So, naturally, this individual lacks knowledge. But when he is plowing his land, he knows exactly where his property ends and his neighbor's begins. He also knows that he can plow a little bit into the neighbor's land, and by doing so, he could increase his own harvest. But he decides not to do it. Not because he has knowledge that he had acquired at school but because this man has a conscience."

"Conscience," Ramon repeated. "I understand that, but it doesn't mean the same thing as wisdom, does it? But tell me, Professor, if this man lacks knowledge, is it natural that he may also lack wisdom?"

"Socrates created an interesting formula three hundred years before Christ that says goodness equals wisdom, and evil equals ignorance. That is to say, when we act with malice in mind, we lack wisdom. Or we lack knowledge of the good. Do you have paper and a pen so I can show it to you in writing?" She quickly drew out a little diagram:

Goodness   Wisdom

Evil   Ignorance

Evil is ignorance to apply wisdom.

Ramon studied the paper a moment. "What do you mean when you say 'goodness'?"

"I am referring to piety, charity, kindness, and clemency. All of those words mean goodness," said Lucia. "Evil means malice, blasphemy, malevolence, slander, and the like."

Ramon paused again with his clipping. His mind worked overtime considering the implications of Lucia's diagram and definitions. Finally, he asked, "Professor, how do we really know when we are acting right or wrong if behavior changes with cultures and time? Sometimes we don't even know anymore what is good and what is evil. You know how most of the time when we make mistakes we say 'Oh, I'm sorry. I didn't know what I was doing' or 'I didn't mean anything bad.' But either way, we can cause a lot of harm if we lack goodness and wisdom, isn't that right?"

"You're definitely on the right track," Lucia assured. "The universal law for peace of mind is to think with goodness and stay away from evil and ignorance. I don't care how insignificant the bad choice of conduct is because the moment we hurt someone, we have done evil.

MARÍA ELENA PELLINEN

Unfortunately, there are a lot of people with knowledge who take advantage of it to cause harm to other people, and they manage to get away with it, like in both movies."

"Okay," Ramon said. "Okay. I think I get it. You always add to my education every time you come in." He lifted the apron off and gestured to the mirror.

"And every time I come in," Lucia smiled, "you subtract from my unruly mop. It looks wonderful. I'll be back soon for another one of your Hollywood haircuts!"

26

Worker or Professional

APPLAUSE GREETED LUCIA. She beamed in the warmth of admiration from the assembled group inside Kat's Café. Her audience had grown from a small circle of friends and students in the beginning to close to fifty. When she cancelled a session because of family or professional obligations, the next session always had *increased* attendance, as Lucia said, "Therefore demonstrating the theory of supply and demand."

She took her place on the elevated corner stage that Kat had installed especially for these evenings. "A very good evening to you, and *buenas noches*, my dear colleagues. I am very glad to be here tonight on this wonderful Saturday evening with all of you. As you may know, I was not here last Saturday because I celebrated my twin daughters' birthday, and I also went to New York for a teacher's conference. What a city—the crowds, the buildings! As I was walking right on Fifth Avenue, I wondered, how does it feel to live way up there on the fifty-second floor of any one of those buildings?" Lucia chuckled lightly. "I must confess to you that I felt an instant rush of depression, and I was glad that I was only one more tourist in that incredible city. Did you know that Manhattan has more than a dozen mental hospitals? I wonder why?" Her arch question was met by appreciative laughter.

"Before I start, I want to thank you from the bottom of my heart for being here one more time with me at Kat's Café." The applause was surprisingly loud.

Lucia gestured to the audience to settle down. She said, "Let me tell you about the best workmanship I experienced in the city. I was dining with a couple of professors at the hotel restaurant. A guy by the name of Carlos Nava was our waiter. The quality of his service was amazing. I told him, 'I am very happy to see your quality of service as you attend your customers.' And he said to me, "Thank you, Ma'am. Just doing my job." I complimented him again on his comprehensive and enthusiastic work, and Carlos said to me, 'I ought to do it with enthusiasm because if I don't, what I am doing here every day for eight hours? Just imagine if I worked against my will. By the time I got back to my family, most likely, I would be in a horrible mood, and that wouldn't be fair to my wife and three children.'

"I was so impressed with his attitude that I left a letter complimenting both Carlos and the manager because the manager is doing his job, having staff like Carlos. So, after this anecdote, it makes sense to study tonight with all of you the difference between *worker* and *professional*."

"Tell me about it," murmured Kat from behind the counter.

"Let's define our terms," Lucia began. "The word *employee* itself tells us that this is a person who is *employed* for a job or task with the expectations of being paid. And a *professional* implies someone who has a profession or career, which rather than a single job describes a path constructed of many cooperative tasks resulting in an overall goal. Let's learn from Plato, our best-known philosopher from antiquity. Plato divided his utopia in three groups of people: the working class, the guardian class, and the ruler class. Among the working class, Plato includes all of those individuals who are productive to society for the exchange of pay. The craftsman for Plato was a legal citizen who had all the privileges the government can afford for its working class."

Cesar, a young man who joined the group a few sessions ago, asked, "What about Socrates? Socrates did not accept any kind of salary. How did he survive?"

"That is a very good observation, Cesar. And for our new guests, please feel free to join in the conversation, just like Cesar. We are all friends here." Lucia led quick applause for Cesar. "Now, continuing with Cesar's question, in the case of Socrates, he had plenty of very good friends who were willing to house and feed him.

"One day Socrates had to apologize to the jury in front of the judges. But I must tell you, while our modern jury has only twelve citizens, during Socrates's day, the jury was composed of every citizen that could be part of the audience. Some days, juries were up to five hundred people." There were gasps and low whistles in response to this amazing factoid.

Continuing, Lucia said, "That day, Socrates spoke of all the benefits that he had received as a legal citizen, and these benefits were similar to the rights of his parents and grandparents. The benefits also included his school education and the privilege to be legally married. These benefits were not only for him but also for all the rest of the legal Athenian citizens."

"I'm confused. You're saying that every legal citizen was a craftsman?" asked Robert, a newcomer.

"Ah," exclaimed Lucia. "We did digress with Socrates and his benefits. Yes, the craftsman were the teachers, shoemakers, butchers, bakers, candlemakers, salesmen, farmers, masons, painters, poets, doctors, engineers, lawyers, religious ministers, and so on. That is to say, anyone who belongs to the working class or 'arte,' and from this term, we get the words 'artesian' and 'artisan' because Plato wanted everyone to practice his craft as an artist.

"Now allow me to relate this 'arte' with Carlos, the waiter that I met in New York. Plato would have told me that my waiter was a craftsman full of pride and civic responsibility."

"I'm sorry, Professor," said a rather large woman down front. "I'm lost. When you started, you said we would learn the difference between worker and professional. Now you're talking about craftsmen and artists or something. Where does a plain old employee come in?"

"Maybe it's because I'm tired from my week," Lucia said by way of apology. "I don't mean to be flip, but if you are asking me who are the employees, I will tell you that anyone who has been employed is an employee."

The large woman harrumphed.

Cesar asked, "Getting back to Plato, who were the professionals in that society?"

"According to Plato, the professionals are the people like you and me who work for the community, regardless of whatever job we may do. I know some of you may only make the minimum wage, and I know everyone would like to make a lot more, but if you are proud of the work you do, then you deserve to be included among the professionals of the highest quality with civic and ethical consciousness," Lucia explained.

"I'm sorry, Professor, but I just don't see how, if I am making minimum wage, I am going to call myself a *professional*." the large woman demanded.

"I understand your question," Lucia said patiently. "And there are those for whom a job is simply a paycheck. But regardless of your pay grade, if you are focused on the quality of your work, and it is for the good of society, then you are a professional. My dear friend Dr. Peter Koestenbaum explains this point in one of his books. He says one must make sure to teach children to obey because when the child obeys with a willing attitude, the child is developing leadership skills as he learns to be of service to the others."

The large woman slapped her purse in a gesture of exasperation. "Obeying—following—teaches leadership skills?" she sneered. "What kind of mustard are you using on that baloney?"

"Wait! I think I got it," exclaimed the girl next to Cesar. "Are you saying that if a student willingly obeys the rules and follows the parent or teacher, then they are open to learning, which teaches them knowledge, which then leads to comprehending leadership?"

"Bravo!" cheered Lucia.

"You could have said that in the first place," complained the large woman. "And what you are saying sounds wonderful, but the truth is that teachers today aren't always good, and if my kids are any example, all they do is send home a shipload of homework that I get the joy of dealing with."

Lucia agreed. "You are correct. Unfortunately many teachers have not learned the real philosophical purpose of homework. It should reinforce classroom concepts and teach the importance of self-starting. Parents should be there for support but not necessarily to be experts in all the subjects. If my kids come to me with questions about trigonometry or calculus, all I will be able to say is *Ayayay*! The parent's obligation is to make sure that the children do their daily homework. When we persuade our children to do homework, we are teaching them to develop a leader's mentality as the children learn to be of service.

"For me, it is clear that Carlos, our New York waiter, grew up obeying his parents and doing his homework, and I was very happy to have met him as a very proud and mature worker."

Lucia's mind wandered. Thoughts of what her son and daughters were doing now took her concentration. Coming back to the present, she looked at her expectant audience. She sighed. "Forgive me. I must excuse myself." She tittered in self-awareness. "To tell you the truth, I am very tired, and after a week in the east, I am behind a whole three hours. Please visit with Kat and continue enjoying your coffee and cookies while I go home to put my feet up."

Lucia had just locked her car door in the driveway when a voice nearby shouted, "Goal!". Lucia's heart leapt into her throat, but it was only Gilberto, her longtime neighbor and fellow Mexican immigrant, leaning over the hedge. His face beamed, and his handlebar mustache twitched. He wore a jersey with the Mexican national colors: green, white, and red. He practically danced a *tarantella*. "Did you see the World Cup game just now? Did you see how lucky we are?"

"I just heard on the car radio." Lucia replied. "As Mexicans, we feel very proud for our winning team. But, you know, luck had very little to do with winning. These players were not just throwing dice, nor is it a matter of random chance. I'm very tired now, but how would you like to come tomorrow night when my husband is home so we can have a cup of coffee and talk more about the great game?"

"That would be wonderful!" Gilberto answered.

"See you tomorrow night, my dear neighbor, and please bring Miriam, your beautiful wife," Lucia said, anxious to get to the comfort of her soft bed.

"We are delighted!" Gilberto called after her. "I look forward to your philosophical explanation of random chance, Lucia! Goooooaaaal!" he shouted again.

"*Ay caramba!*" Lucia murmured, going in the side door.

27

Drunk or Sober

D URING LUCIA'S LAST ethics class, she had dealt with temperance and the importance of when or where or how much of drinking alcohol would make sense. Her new newspaper column was dedicated to Mathew, the son of one of her students in that class.

Drunk or Sober

Have you ever wondered why the legal drinking age in the United States is twenty-one years old? Eighteen-year-olds can enlist in the armed forces, vote, get married, have children, go to jail for life, run his or her own business, and even become very rich. So why can they not drink alcohol legally until the age of twenty-one?

All of these questions were the theme of one of my philosophy lectures. The students offered their points of view and spoke of alternatives that mixed philosophy with religion and politics with history. A new student, an older student, eventually stood up and filled the room with her firm, stern voice.

Her name is Mary, and I remember precisely what she said: "If you allow me, I am going to tell you why in the United States the legal drinking age is twenty-one.

"We all know that many young people make the choice to drink several years earlier than the law permits. But what most of us don't know is that the brain is not completely developed until after the age of twenty or twenty-one. If you have not yet developed the capacity to reason and think critically, then how can you effectively consider how you will operate under the influence of alcohol?

"The school of medicine at Colombia University in New York participated in a series of investigations that concluded that people who start drinking between the ages of fifteen and twenty years of age run the risk to become lifetime alcoholics at twice the rate as those who start drinking after they are twenty-one years old.

"Don't say that people drink because they drink, as if you were saying that people study because they study or buy a car or go on a date. Any of these choices represent maturity and responsibility. To drink alcoholic beverages is not a norm because those that get drunk need to know that their behavior is not acceptable because alcohol has already altered their chances for a good and happy life.

"It has been nearly twenty-seven years since my son Mathew was born. We named him Mathew because that name means 'given by God.' Mathew grew up being a great kid, a great student, athletic and progressive. While young, he volunteered his time in all kinds of projects for our community. He studied very hard in order to be accepted at the Naval Academy. Unfortunately, all of his expectations of a happy life were destroyed by a drunken man with a license suspended five times."

At that moment, the classroom was filled with quiet echoes of grief. Mary stayed quiet for several seconds, as did the entire class. It was as if everyone present shared a moment of silence on Mathew's behalf. After those long seconds, Mary continued telling everyone about alcoholism and its consequences. Now, in every person's heart, each word Mary spoke was now dedicated to Mathew.

"Did you know that the half of the young people in the United States drink alcohol? The National Center of Addiction and Drugs at Columbia University tells us that alcohol kills 6.5 times more young people that any other addiction to drugs."

After Mary finished, she sat down, and I continued my lecture, telling them that we need to change our social norms so the mothers like Mathew's mom don't have to suffer the deaths of their children because of the irresponsibility of the drunk driver. If we change those norms, we won't incur all the expenses of trying to cure the sickness caused by alcohol.

Commit yourselves, those of you who are not yet twenty-one, to stay away from alcohol. Know that is better if you don't start. And those of you that are of legal drinking age, if you choose to drink, drink responsibly.

I would like to add other statistics to Mary's comments. Did you know that adolescents illegally consume 17 percent of all alcoholic beverages sold? And alcoholic beverages consumed by the adult public generate more than $23.8 billion dollars in sales? Now you can see why the alcohol industry can pay for all those ads in magazines and on television, convincing the youth of our country to drink alcohol. They persuade ironically with an image of alcoholic consumption that suggests it is the way to better health and happiness, the same way that the tobacco industry works.

Thus, my dear reader, I hope that you can persuade yourself or your minors to stay away from alcohol and above all from drinking and driving.

As always, yours truly,
Lucia. Con Amor!

Completing her column, Lucia wished it could be published time and again so those that did not read it today could read it tomorrow.

Success or Failure

L UCIA'S NEXT-DOOR NEIGHBOR Gilberto moonwalked down her porch, triumphant ly dropping to his knees with a loud, "Goooooooaaaal!" as Lucia opened her front door. He still wore his Mexican National Team Jersey.

His wife Miriam bore a pained expression. "He won't give it to me to launder. He says I'll wash the luck out of it," she explained.

Lucia welcomed them in with a laugh. Inside, Gary greeted them with a tray of pastries. "Coffee, tea, or what you will?" he offered.

Coffee, please," said Miriam.

"Nada, gracias," said Gilbert.

"Tea for me," Lucia said. "If I drink coffee, I will philosophize all night, and we must have pity on Gary." Gary headed toward the kitchen, concealing a grimace.

As they sat, Lucia said, "You know, Gilberto, I have been thinking about what you said last night, celebrating the 'good luck' of our team having won the World Cup. I told you that in those events there is not so much random chance like the random chance we experience when we play the slot machine at a casino."

"Yes, but the real important thing is Mexico takes the World Cup!" he roared.

"Calm down, sweetheart," Miriam said, patting his thigh.

Lucia plowed forward. "Well, what I wanted to tell you is that in this very competitive sport, what counts are power, force, vigor, self-control, concentration, and so on. All of these are the virtues of the winner."

Miriam asked, "Is this the definition of virtue that I learned in your philosophy class? Aristotle's definition? The one that says that virtue is a kind of excellence that improves human quality?"

"Nicely put, Miriam." Lucia said.

"And we have the best virtue-istic *fútbol* team in the world—*Fútbol Mexicano*!" said Gilbert.

"Honey, cool it on the football, okay? You need to be thinking about the virtues you need to win in your job. What do you have to say about that, Lucia?" asked Miriam.

"Gilbert, I think Miriam wants you to hear this," Lucia said. "So I will use some of the points made by my dear friend Dr. Peter Koestenbaum. In his book *Leadership: The Inner Side of Greatness,* he uses the Olympic symbol to demonstrate how one can become a leader and a winner.

"First of all, picture the Olympic symbol in your mind, the famous five overlapping circles, three on the top and two on the bottom. Here, I'll draw them," said Lucia, hopping up to grab paper and pen. "Now, inside each circle we are going to write one word, starting with *Person,* then *Family, Work, Civic Responsibilities,* and *Finances,* like this."

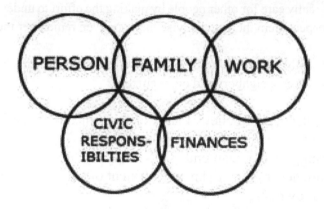

"Now let's draw inside of each circle a rhombus or diamond. On the top angle of the diamond, we'll put the word *ethics*; on the bottom angle, *courage*; on the left side, *reality*; on the right, *vision*, like this."

"And each diamond in each of the five circles has the same words?" asked Miriam.

"Exactly, Miriam. But today we are going to analyze only the side dedicated to the person. And that person is you or Gilbert or yours truly."

Lucia pointed to her diagram. "The purpose of *ethics* is to discover the best and the worst in each person. When we are sick, we take our temperature, and we know that the higher the fever, the sicker we are. In philosophy, that temperature is taken with a 'humanitarian thermometer' that indicates our moral and ethical health and teaches us to rid ourselves of vices by adding more virtues into our daily conduct. In order to apply this remedy, each one of us must answer the following questions:

"Do I really care for other people by making the effort to understand and respect them, help and advise them, or even remember them?

"Do I really know how to be kind and compassionate with friends and relatives, neighbors and other citizens?

"As a person, do I believe I am excellent, mediocre, good, or bad? What grade can I give my test ethical conduct?

"Returning to our diamond. Let's analyze *courage*. According to Plato, we are never going to know the extent of our courage if we don't confront our own fears."

"But, what about all of those bullies that cross our paths all the time?" asked Gilbert.

"Bullies?" asked Lucia. "As an adult you deal with bullies?"

"He doesn't deal with bullies, Lucia," Miriam said, giving Gilbert a light slap across the shoulder. "He's talking about our son Fernando. There is a bullying problem at the middle school."

"I see. That is a problem. But, let's not confuse *courage* with bullying and arrogance, or its opposite—cowardliness, timidity, and weakness of character. Do you know that *courage* is the perfect ingredient to develop equanimity of character and the right tool to solve all our self-created problems?"

"You are so right about that," Miriam said.

"First of all, we must try not to feel overwhelmed with our problems because a problem always contains a solution," Lucia noted. "On the other hand, our concern is no longer a problem once it has become a situation, and situations become more bearable by applying strength and resignation.

"When my good friend's mom became ill, my friend had lots of related problems. She had to fire a nurse, which caused her to have to take over her mom's care until she found an appropriate replacement. Then she needed a double shift of nurses as her mom got sicker and sicker, until one day she died. Sadly, her mom's death ended all of those accumulated problems instantly. Now she was left with only one thing to do and that was the application of acceptance and resignation. Do you know what I mean, Miriam?"

"Yes, Lucia, I do."

"Now, going back to the importance of being conscious of ethical behavior: Imagine a young man waiting for his mom to get home from work. His mom pulls her car into the driveway, and the son asks if she plans to go out tonight. She replies, 'Are you kidding? I just want to take off my shoes and sit for a while.' So the son says, 'So I could drive your car tonight. Am I right?' By making this jump in logic, the son has done what I call *ethically pulling the carpet from underneath his mother*. If you were to give the son a grade for ethical behavior, what grade would you give him, Gilbert?"

Gilbert looked up suddenly and exclaimed, "Huh?" Miriam rolled her eyes. Gilbert said, "Don't blame me. I'm still waiting for her to say something about how luck doesn't count."

"I would flunk him immediately," Miriam said, her eye on Gilbert.

Lucia chuckled. "Now, let's analyze *vision*. Visualize an acute angle. Put yourself at the point, and imagine the open side is your field of vision, limited by your ethics and your acceptance of inspiration. If you allow your ethics to develop toward perfection and you become more and more open to inspiration, the angle will continue opening more and more.

"Let me tell you a little story. A man decided to go into business by himself, but then he thought that if his cousin could join him, the business could be stronger and grow. He invited him, but hi cousin said no. He did not want to invest his little savings. The man thanked him for his honesty and opened his business all by himself. Twenty years passed. The man became a millionaire and improved the life of hundreds of employees. His cousin's financial situation never improved, and he sits every day feeling sorry for himself because he lacked *vision* when the opportunity that presented twenty years ago. The moral of the story is simple. As the nineteenth-century German philosopher Georg Hegel said very well, 'Nothing is ever accomplished without enthusiasm.'"

Gilbert had been studying the diagram. "What about *reality*?" he asked.

"Yes, the fourth side. Gilbert, the purpose of *reality* is to know how to manage time properly. Lamenting the loss of all of those choices that were never made—such as the choice to have gone to college, have bought a home, put money in the bank, and even exercise and good nutrition—only give the poor person several reasons to be depressed instead of knowing that every day we can discover endless possibilities for better choices that could start now. And for that we must always keep in mind that time has three very important links. That is to say: I am my past, I am my present, and I am my future."

"Professor, that reminds me of a story told by my psychology teacher. Do we still have time, speaking of time?" Miriam asked.

"I do if you do," Lucia said, noting Gary stifling a yawn.

Miriam noted the yawn too. She said, "I'll make this quick. A man goes to see a therapist and says, 'I don't know what to do. I want to go to college, but I am thirty-five years old.' The therapist asks, 'How old will you be when you finish your degree?' The guy thinks a minute and replies, 'With my full-time job and my family responsibilities, it will take at least ten years. I'd be forty-five years old.' Then the therapist asked, 'And how old will you be in ten years if you do not go to school?' The man answers, 'Hmm, forty-five!'"

Even sleepy Gary laughed at that one. They rose, hugged, and headed toward the door.

"One more thing before you go," Lucia said. "Back to our diamond: how close do you think you are to winning an ethical Olympic medal? Remember, no one but you can truly evaluate your own ethical scores."

"We'll work on it," Gilbert answered. "And sometime I really want to hear what you say about luck because with our team to win the World Cup, there had to be a lot of luck, along with God and all the gods of the Aztecs throwing all their good will our way."

"He'll get better. I promise," laughed Miriam.

And with that, the neighbors wished each other a very good night.

29

An Apple or a Car

" **J**ANE, YOU MISSED the turn," Lucia said as they crossed the arterial road on their way back from shopping.

Jane remained focused dead ahead. "Something I want to see," she said. "It will only take a few minutes."

Lucia knew exactly where she was headed—to Auto Dealer Row. Some new models came out in the last few weeks, and Jane's obsession was new cars. She didn't need a new car. Jane just wanted to look.

A few days later, Lucia met with her childhood friend Tobias Renquist, now Father Renquist, the priest. They met to talk periodically, sort of a friendly exchange of ideas with the vague goal of gaining either a new slant on Christian philosophy for Lucia or a homily topic for Tobias.

With the weather warm and sunny, they sat down on the bench in the little enclosed garden between the church and the rectory. "How are Gary, Sam, the twins, and Alexandria?" Tobias inquired.

"All are well. The kids are growing like weeds," Lucia told him. "I leave for work in the morning, and when I come home, they've grown another inch. And how about you? How are things here?"

Tobias sighed. "As we have discussed, the hierarchy needs to get its act together. They have completely forgotten the purpose of God's church. They've gone into circle-the-wagons mode. No one takes responsibility for all the harm."

"You sound ready to leave," Lucia said.

"No," Tobias assured her. "Better to work from within than without. But what shall we talk about today? I don't have a lot of time. I have a young couple coming in for pre-marriage counsel. They've been together for five years, so it's just a formality. What am I going to say to them since they know each other so well already?"

"Temptation is everywhere," Lucia observed. An idea struck her. "I think I may have an idea for a sermon. I think I hit on a way to revisit the Genesis story."

Tobias grinned tightly. "Been there, done that. I think over my career as a priest, I have found hundreds of ways to relate that tale."

"Just give me a minute to brainstorm the details for you and then you can decide," Lucia said. She got up to pace. She often walked when she talked, and she thought her walking increased her circulation and therefore improved her thinking. "Okay, listen to this," she began.

"As you know Adam and Eve had it all. They had so much. They had no idea what it was to be cold, hungry, thirsty, sick, or afraid. Nor had they ever seen any natural disasters because they were surrounded by peace and the weather was so perfect that they could spend all day naked up to their neck enjoying everything that the Lord had procured for them. Adam and Eve were intelligent. They understood very well the Lord's instructions concerning *obedience*. In other words, they knew that they had complete freedom, except that they could not touch the apple tree. I don't know why it had to be apples. It could have been oranges or plums, but that day the Lord must have been in an apple mood."

"Lucia, we talked many times about details that bear no relation to the meaning of a story," Tobias said. "I don't hear anything I have not heard bazillions of times before."

"I haven't gotten to the analogy, so just wait. So one day, Eve strolls by the apple tree, the same way we look at brand-new cars for sale."

Suddenly, Tobias brightened. Lucia went on. "All of a sudden, the serpent gets close to Eve and begs her to taste the apple. He tells her he has been waiting for her for several days. All he wants her to do is to take a bite as a favor to him. Just the same way a salesman seduces a customer to test-drive that shiny brand-new car."

Pretending to be the salesman, Lucia jangled her keys in front of Tobias. "Here are the keys. C'mon. Help me out. The boss is watching. Let me show him I'm doing my job." Lucia switched to the sibilant snake. "C'mon, Eve. Just touch the apple, do it for me."

"I think I've used the 'just touch it' metaphor before."

"Be patient and listen," Lucia admonished. "Eve says, 'To touch is not to eat, right?' And the salesman says, 'Driving the car does not mean that you're actually buying it, right?' So Eve takes the apple in her hand. It's lovely—red and shiny and perfect in shape with a delicious aroma. The customer slides behind the wheel. The car is shiny and new, inside and out. And it has that *new car smell*! The serpent encourages, 'Taste

MARÍA ELENA PELLINEN

it. Taste it. Where's the harm in a little taste?' The salesman says, 'Just give it a quick spin. Where's the harm in a test drive?' With the apple so close to her lips, Eve cannot resist taking a bite. Sitting behind the wheel, the customer cannot resist starting up and pulling onto the street. Eve swoons down to a grassy mound, mesmerized by the taste of the forbidden apple. The customer says, 'I'll take it,' mesmerized by the smooth ride and deft handling. The customer signs the sales contract. Adam finds Eve on the grassy mound, nibbling at the apple. He freaks! 'Woman! Are you out of your mind? What are you doing?' Eve holds out the fruit to him and says, 'Don't say anything and taste this incredible fruit!' The apple is so shiny and red and smells wonderful. Adam reasons that since Eve already had a bite, the damage is done. He takes a big bite. The customer's husband sees his wife pull the new car into the driveway. He freaks! 'Oh my god, what are you doing buying this car?' The man's wife says, 'Don't say a word and get into this amazing car.' Her husband sees how shiny and aerodynamic the car is, and it has that new car smell! He reasons that the car has been bought, so the damage is done. He gets in and takes the car for a spin around the neighborhood.

"Then, all of a sudden, with the flavor of the apple still in Adam and Eve's mouths, the Lord arrives and berates them, 'I can see that you have disobeyed me. Both of you have eaten from the forbidden fruit. Now, at once you must leave paradise forever!' Eve falls to her knees and tries to explain to the Lord the weakness of her character, saying she only did what the serpent told her. Just like the customer tells herself she was only trying to help the salesman to sell a car. 'And you, Adam, what can you tell me?' demands the Lord. And Adam whines, 'This woman that you have given me really pushed me to bite the apple!' And the husband reasons that his wife bought the car, so he has to drive it. And the Lord intones, 'Adam, not only have you disobeyed me, but then you blame Eve! You have made the mistake of your lifetime. You knew Eve committed a sin, and you had time to reflect upon her conduct and still went ahead and knowingly you made the choice to disobey.

"Thus, the two sinners were thrown out of paradise because they ate the forbidden fruit, *deliberately disobeying the Lord*. And now the modern couple is condemned to pay for a car they can barely afford. Who then committed the biggest sin in either case, the man or the woman? Two people with the same moral background committed the sin. And this explains to us that there is no masculine or feminine sin because a sin is a sin. The challenge now is not to behave like either one of these two but to have the courage to follow social and divine norms in order to be able to enjoy peace of mind and tranquility of spirit during one's lifetime."

Tobias thought hard, considering all Lucia said. *This could make an intriguing sermon,* he thought. Turning to Lucia, he said, "So, your friend Jane is looking at cars again?"

MARÍA ELENA PELLINEN

30

Envy or Jealousy

SUNDAY MORNING IN the park, just before eight, soccer, picnicking, Frisbee throwing, and dog walking have yet to begin. On the west border of the park is the tree where Lucia loves to sit and read, observe, and counsel—counseling is her favorite activity. Her altruistic advice, for the most part, is spot on, and her reputation has spread. She came early today. Some bit of intuition made her think, with great anticipation, that someone would seek her help early on.

A few individuals she knew strolled by, and she greeted them as they passed, but none stopped for counseling. She felt her heart rate increase as her frustration grew. A city bus stopped nearby. Three passengers got off, a woman and two men. One of the men, tall and blond-haired, spotted her and sprinted toward her. Lucia breathed a long sigh of relief. Her purpose returned.

He arrived breathless from his run. "Professor, I am so glad to find you here. Alice told me that this is your favorite spot on Sunday mornings, and I see that she was right."

The man bent over and rested his arms on his knees, catching his breath.

"Robert. What's the matter?" Lucia asked. "You didn't have to run. I'm not going anywhere."

He plopped next to her on the bench. "Jessica's gone. I've lost her. She's taken up with a guy who is so bad for her." He hid his face in his hands, stifling tears. Lucia patted his back gently, motherly. "We dated more than three years, and we were supposed to get married in the fall." Robert sniffed. "I am going to get her back from that man."

Gently, Lucia asked, "Have you spoken with her?"

He gritted his teeth. "No, but I'll get her back because she's mine."

"Robert!" Lucia said firmly. "Jessica is her own person despite being your object of desire. You don't own her."

Robert relented. "Yeah, I know," he said.

"I think you are confused between *jealousy* and *envy*. You may be very upset because she left you, and you are also very angry because she is already with someone else. Am I right?" Looking away from her, Robert nodded curtly. "All right," she continued, "allow me to show you, philosophically speaking, what is happening to you. Thomas Hobbes explained quite clearly the origin of envy, saying that 'when there is only one thing, but two people want to have it, that is the birth of envy and therefore of the enemy.'"

Robert leaned forward in thought. Lucia thought he still listened. She went on. "There was a young woman who lived in a second-floor apartment. From her window, she could see her boyfriend walking toward her for almost the length of the block. One of those days while she watched her boyfriend approach, she saw him give a hug to a strange woman who also hugged him back with a great deal of affection. They hugged not once, but hugged again. The strange woman was blonde, slender, pretty, and tall. They chatted for a while showing a great deal of joy. Then, from a plastic bag, he gave her a package that resembled a box of chocolates, and not only did she smile, but she even hugged and kissed it. They embraced one more time and said good-bye. The two of them walked away in opposite directions, turning to each other once more to wave another good-bye."

Robert shifted. Satisfied she had his full attention, Lucia continued her story. "Meanwhile, the girlfriend in the second-floor window got angrier and angrier. But when her boyfriend arrived, she pretended to be happy to see him and ready to spend quality time with her fiancé. However, after that love scene, she couldn't pretend to be as happy as always. So she complained of a headache and told him that she would prefer to be alone.

"During the next visit, she told him that she was very busy. Two days later, he brought her a beautiful bouquet of flowers. Still, she did not forget that love scene that she had seen with her own two eyes. She canceled again. He wondered what the matter was with her and why she cancelled every date. He decided to ask her if anything was wrong. She responded in a fine fury. 'You ask me if I am fine? How is it possible you can be such a hypocrite and cynic and continue behaving as if nothing happened?'

"Completely nonplussed, the boyfriend asked, 'Wait a minute, what are you talking about? I don't understand what you're saying! What do you mean by hypocrite and cynic?'

MARÍA ELENA PELLINEN

"So she challenged him, 'Are you going to tell me you forgot that great big hug and kiss that you gave to that blond girl in the middle of the street?'

"The boyfriend remained at sea. 'I did what? What are you talking about?' he asked.

"The girlfriend had to hold her emotions tightly to keep from losing it. 'Oh my god, don't you remember anything? I saw both of you from my window.' She described the day, the hour, the place, and even the shirt that he was wearing. Finally he remembered the encounter.

"'Her name is Linda,' he told her. 'She found me on Facebook. We went to high school together ten years ago, and she invited me to the class reunion. Our favorite teacher is retiring. I couldn't go to the reunion, and I asked if she would give the teacher a book for me.'

"The girlfriend became so embarrassed. She asked, 'The package that you gave her wasn't a box of chocolates? From a distance, I thought it looked like chocolates. And she hugged you.'

"The boyfriend said, 'We hadn't seen each other in ten years. We hugged. As friends. And that was that.' So the girlfriend sniffed back a tear, and they pledged their love to each other because they were truly in love, and they both knew that jealousy nearly destroyed what they held so dear."

Robert smiled wanly. Lucia knew he heard the message beneath her story. "Remember," Lucia added, *jealousy is the inability to posses the other's freedom*. Lucia took Robert's hand and held it gently. "Robert," she said with obvious caring, "in your case, your girlfriend left you, and as Plato said, 'appearances are the worst enemy.' The young lady of my story used her imagination beyond limits. She had to learn that our senses are very capable of deceiving and that it is necessary 'to know how to see,' meaning to see with the eyes of the intellect.

"When in doubt, it is important to ask. Asking questions is never wrong. But when we allow our insecure thoughts to take over, we may take everything we see with uncritical eyes as the whole of reality. "Oh jealousy, Shakespeare's green-eyed monster." Lucia gripped Robert's hand tightly, lovingly. "In your case, dear Robert, that ex-girlfriend has done you a favor leaving you before she married you and had children."

Finally, Robert looked directly at her. "Do you really think so, Professor?"

"Yes!" Lucia assured emphatically. "Now you need to cross the line of doubt and let her go. Very soon, you will recognize that she did not love you. Without true love, what would be the purpose of sharing your existence with someone that does not love you?

Another person, a sad, young woman approached and hesitated nearby. *Another person needing my counsel,* Lucia thought. She released Robert's hand, saying, "Robert, take care of yourself. Pay attention to your graduate work, visit your old friends, spend quality time with your parents and your family, and come and join us next Saturday at Kat's Café."

"Excellent suggestions, Professor." Robert rose and looked across the park. Lucia's counsel refreshed and renewed him, and his former girlfriend was rapidly becoming a memory. Two pretty girls unrolled towels on the broad lawn, preparing to sun themselves. Robert, his attention riveted, said, "Thank you, Professor. Can I bring a date?"

MARÍA ELENA PELLINEN

31

Honest or Shameless

A T BEANS 'N' Such Coffee Bar, Claudia tore open a package of sweetener and added it to her coffee, along with nearly half a cup of half-and-half. "You asked the barista to put a tall cup of coffee into the next size up cup," Lucia observed. "Why did you do that?"

Claudia stirred her coffee, replaced the lid, and dropped several more sweetener packs into her purse. "It's called a ghetto latte," she explained. "Why pay an extra two fifty when I can add the milk myself?"

"What about the creamer for other customers?" Lucia worried, looking around to see if they were watched. She felt proximity guilt.

"They have lots in the back. They expect people to take it." She and Lucia sat down in oversized armchairs near the window. "Oh my god, Professor, if I could tell you what I just experienced!" she said intensely. "I was in the Grocery Outlet on Third, and I couldn't believe what I saw. There was this mother and a father with two little girls of maybe five and seven years old. They were all literally *stealing*. The father was putting things in his jacket pockets. The mother was putting them inside of her big purse, and the little girls put stolen stuff in their own little backpacks. I couldn't believe that they were so calm about it. In the end of all of that, they paid for a few things and left the place like the most honest people on earth."

Lucia shook her head regretfully. "How sad that those parents are already instilling such horrible vices in those poor little kids. Soon they will think that they are doing the right thing because their parents are very proud of them for following their direction."

They sipped their coffees pensively, momentarily in their own thoughts. Lucia set her cup on the table between them and began, "You know, Claudia, lately I have been thinking of developing a scale from one to ten that could actually measure our sense of integrity and honesty. The number 10 would be the mark for the highest and best conduct going down as the conduct deteriorates from honesty to dishonesty, and in the case of your recent experience from honesty to thievery."

"That sounds interesting. Who would do the rating? I'm not sure I trust the government to do it," Claudia said. "And would you take into account parental influence, peer influence, that sort of thing?"

"You would have to factor in the very education that children receive from their parents or guardians," Lucia said. "As you saw, those two poor little girls are growing up believing that stealing is good because when they steal they receive praise and reward from their parents. And those same parents tell them to be sure no one sees them not because stealing is wrong, but because they can be caught. According to David Hume, all our knowledge is fundamentally empirical. That is to say, everything that we experience leaves physical or ideal impressions in our brain."

Claudia listened intently, considering all Lucia said. "Then, Professor, in the case of these little girls, if they continue on this path, it is going to be very difficult for them to learn that to steal is a vice and that honesty is a virtue because this behavior is engrained. Am I right, Professor?"

"Absolutely right, Claudia. You have been paying attention in your psychology classes."

Claudia asked, "Could we say that those little girls will never know how to be virtuous?"

"No, Claudia," Lucia responded. "No, there is always hope. But, unfortunately, all of those impressions from bad habits that they have been acquiring never will be forgotten. But, they could be substituted if the children have an epiphany that their behavior is wrong and then look for redemption while in search of a better life."

Seeing her friend and student puzzling over the broadening ethics question, Lucia said, "Let me give another example. Imagine that yours truly, Lucia, is invited to give a conference at one of those big eastern universities, and before the audience comes in, I want to make sure that the projector works because I have to use it in my seminar. So I go and check it out, and while I test the equipment, I discover that in that classroom, there are three identical remote controls. I only need one, but I remember that the remote in my house has gone missing. And I think since the university has three, no one will miss one if I took it because they still have two. And they probably have more in an equipment room, and they probably expect people to take them. I haven't had time to go buy one. When I carry my own projector to Kat's Café, I always have to make the changes manually, and I make people sit there and wait for me to make those mechanical changes by hand. To have this additional remote control would solve many of my problems. Claudia, all of my internal talk has resolved into an *idea*. That idea has only one purpose, and that purpose is for me *to possess that remote control*. That means that, besides the empirical knowledge that we accumulate as we learn more and more from experience, we also have the power of the idea before it becomes the chosen action."

"That's not you at all," Claudia said, somewhat appalled at Lucia's self-description. "How did reason form the idea of taking the remote control?"

"Rene Descartes said: *"We are all born good but capable of evil."* Lucia grinned.

"What?" Claudia exclaimed.

"From the greatest German philosopher of the eighteen-century, Immanuel Kant, I have learned that before the *experience* is the *idea*, and before the idea is the *intention* of the idea. That means even though I may not have walked to the classroom with the intention of stealing the remote control, I did walk in with the *potential* of being a thief. Because, according to Kant, before the idea, we find the analysis of the idea. Knowing this theory and knowing how it works has helped me never to say again, 'Oh, I don't know what got into my head' or 'I don't know why I did it' or 'the devil made me do it.'"

Claudia snickered with the recognition of herself in those statements. "Claudia," Lucia asked, "have you ever seen a TV drama with a big strong man is threatening his little, fragile woman?"

"All the time."

"And have you seen how she cries and cries, totally hopeless? Then, from one second to the next, she uses all the energy that she accumulated, and she slaps the man with all her might, and then a second later, she cries even more, saying, 'I am sorry, I am sorry. I don't know what got into me, I am sorry!' Kant would tell us that the little woman, capable of slapping that big man, is also capable of killing him, given the right opportunity."

Claudia became very quiet, considering her own dark thoughts. She went back to the condiment station and returned the extra sweetener packs. Resuming her seat, she asked, "What can we do with those moments of rage that sometimes get to us?"

"There is always *'the intentionality of the idea.'* That is to say, we must be aware that, given the opportunity, we are capable of doing anything. And this is why, if I have become aware that I am capable of stealing the remote control, I am also capable of making several different choices. But I don't have to become a thief and then say, 'I have no idea why I stole the thing since I have never stolen anything before.' So, Claudia, according to Hume, we know that we have our knowledge thanks to our experience."

Taking a sip of her coffee and finding it cold, Lucia realized she had gone on for some time. She asked Claudia if she wanted anything else, and when Claudia didn't, she asked the barista how much a warm up cost. The friendly young man replied, "No charge. Let me get that for you."

Upon returning, Lucia asked, "Claudia, do you speak another language?"

"As a matter of fact, I speak a great deal of French." Claudia smiled, adding, "And I am also learning Italian."

"Then you know how difficult it has been for you to learn what you know. That is to say how difficult it has been to accumulate that learning experience in order to produce knowledge. But then, before that knowledge, we always find the *intention of the idea* to acquire it. This knowledge is based on the willingness to do or not to do a certain thing. *This willingness is precisely the intention that propels our action. Right between the intention and the action we have infinite instants to rescue the goodness and honesty in the intrinsic choice of that particular idea, the real reason we do what we do.* Claudia, do you remember Socrates's most famous quote?"

"I do, Professor, 'Know thyself.'" Claudia felt a good deal of pride.

"That is correct, my dear Claudia, to 'know thyself' means to know oneself inside and out, always keeping track of the *real reason* for which we think, we say, and we do—everything."

Lucia drained the last of her coffee. She took Claudia's empty cup and hers and dropped them in the refuse container. "I hope that those two little girls you saw have the opportunity to know that they were born with *freedom of choice*. For the time being, I am not very optimistic because they are being manipulated and brainwashed by their very dishonest parents. I hope that as they make progress at school with the best of civic education, they may realize the difference between moral and intellectual virtues, and little by little, they may get to the point of knowing the difference between *better or worse, good and evil*."

"Me, too, Professor. Me, too." The women embraced affectionately, and Lucia went on her way. Glancing back at the barista, Claudia saw he was giving her a disapproving look. She mouthed, "Sorry," to him and made a private vow to never again order a ghetto latte.

32

Darkness or Light

"**L**UCIA! LUCIA!"

Where was that coming from, and who called her name? Puzzled, Lucia looked behind her. No one called from that direction. She heard a woman call her name again. Lucia looked back into the door of the pharmacy she had just come from. No. No one in there.

"Yoohoo! Lucia! Over here!" Laura, a tall, slender woman, bounced up and down on the other side of the street, waving her arms. Lucia imagined the woman could easily have qualified for the old Signal Corps. *Put a couple of flags in her hands, and she's good to go*, Lucia thought.

Laura dashed across the street, dodging honking cars. Breathlessly, Laura arrived in front of Lucia and caught her breath. "I am so glad I found you," Laura gasped. "It's imperative we get Vicky to leave her husband. I tried—God knows I tried—and she won't do it!"

"For heaven's sake, Laura. Breathe!" Lucia said, immediately regretting being so abrupt. "What is it that you are trying to tell me?"

Ignoring Lucia's concern, Laura repeated, "You have to help me get Vicky away from that man!"

"We'll work it out, sweetheart, but not right here in the middle of the street. Can you come to my house around four, and we'll put our heads together?"

Sometime later, Sam opened the door and brought Laura in. "Mom, Mrs. Johnson is here," he announced and made himself scarce.

Lucia made a grand entrance with a tray of coffee and freshly baked cookies.

"These are delicious," Laura said, mouth full. "You have to give me the recipe."

"I just slice them off the roll and throw them in the oven," Lucia confessed modestly. "Now, we have about an hour before Gary gets home. Tell me about Vicky."

Laura collected two more warm cookies for her plate. "Well," she said confidentially, "Vicky still lives with Paul, her awful husband. Technically, they're not married, but they do have two children. That would be just fine if they were happy, but they're not. Paul comes home drunk and starts yelling like a mad man and saying, 'Bring me my supper,' and calling her nasty names right in front of the kids." Laura leaned close to Lucia and whispered, "He hits her, Lucia. He does." Tears formed in Laura's eyes as she imagined the living hell poor Vicky endured.

"Does she love this man?" Lucia asked gently.

"No," Laura replied. "We talked, and she told me she doesn't think she has ever loved him. She says she thought she fell in love when they were dating, but now knows she was in love with the idea of being in love. Vicky says she has lost all respect for him.

Laura "I suggested to Vicky that she is more than welcome to come to my house with her children because I have plenty of space where they can stay till they get on their feet. But, she tells me that if Paul found out, he would kill her. Then she tells me that when Paul is not drunk, he is a very nice man, pays for everything, and is a very nice dad. But I never saw that."

"Oh, my dear Laura, that kind of attitude Plato calls 'life in shadows,'" Lucia responded. "Vicky fears the unknown so much that she prefers to live in chaos instead of seeking another alternative. That chaos is the only reality that she knows. The constant high level of stress keeps her from using her imagination to see moving to your house is a wonderful opportunity. With your 'good will,' your idea is a perfect mathematical formula already analyzed and proven because you are 100 percent sure that you are able to keep her in your house. For the time being, you need to ask Vicky to imagine the worst thing that can happen to her if she leaves Paul. Imagination is one of our greatest intellectual skills, and if she is capable of imagining the worst, she also needs to know that the worst never happens and that *evil, as an idea, is nothing*."

Knowing Lucia as well as she does, Laura anticipated the next shoe—a philosophical coda. "Wait a minute, Lucia," she said. "What are you going to tell me about the tons of evil that the world has suffered?"

Lucia's immediate impulse was to stand and address the thought. But she restrained herself and remained sitting. "Very often we may hear someone actually say, 'I hate my boss.' And shortly after that, the boss walks by, and the person says, 'Good morning, boss, how are you?' As you see, that idea of hatred never concerned the boss for a second even though it may have caused a stomachache to the poor woman that held the hateful thought. This is one of the reasons I always give credit to Father Tobias when he says, *'Thou shall not have evil thoughts.'* This is why when you wish evil toward someone, your imagination may cause you more harm than the evil thought may cause harm to the other.

"Vicky needs to leave the shadows behind her in order to see the 'light of day.' Plato would tell her that she needs to be illuminated by the *sunlight.* That means she needs to be capable of discovering the truth of the universal values such as goodness, courage, beauty, justice, and friendship. Those values are lacking in Vicky's miserable existence while she coexists with her drunken and irresponsible husband. All of that will be banished when she dares to see the *light.*

"So," Lucia continued, "Vicky needs to see the difference between the dark side of her life and the clear and healthy reality that awaits her outside of her cave. She needs to be able to step over the line of *doubt* and ask herself a lot of questions that may appear as instant problems yet ultimately lead to solutions. You see, Laura, what has Vicky so confused is that for her, her life is not a problem but a *situation.* This is why she has chosen to stay in a world of clouds, fog, and darkness. Vicky needs to know from us that where there is light, there is life. Light illuminates the source of truth for positive imagination. Keep in mind that goodness is ever-present for all of those that desire to walk away from shadows," Lucia concluded.

Laura's face brightened. "Thank you, Lucia. Your words are ever so poetic, but it is a tangible poetry that I get. Now it's up to me."

"I will do what I can, too," Lucia offered.

"I know. But with Vicky so overwhelmed, let me try first, okay?"

"Of course, but—"

"She and I are best friends," Laura interrupted. "You gave me good tools. I'll get her out of there," she said firmly. "And what kind of cookie dough is this?"

"Store brand. Oatmeal raisin."

"I'll pick some up to bake before I see Vicky. I think they may help the understanding." With that, Laura left on her mission.

33

Horoscopes or Coincidences

"**W**HAT'S SO INTERESTING in the newspaper, Glynis?" Lucia asked.

"Nothing." Glynis folded the paper and tucked it in her satchel.

"Don't be embarrassed. You can find value in just about anything. I have my guilty pleasures. Sometimes when Gary is out and I've finished my work, I turn on the Spanish language channel and watch a *telenovela*." Lucia blushed. "These stories, the acting, and—oh my god—the costumes are so cheesy I can't believe I'm throwing away my valuable time watching such stuff. So, don't be embarrassed. I won't push it any further, but don't be embarrassed about what you read in the newspaper."

Hesitantly, Glynis reached into her satchel for the newspaper. "Just checking out the daily horoscope," she admitted.

"Really?" Lucia said, brightening. "Let me see what mine is!" Lucia slid in beside Glynis and scanned the daily column. "I like that one," she said, pointing to one of the readings.

"Is that your sign?" asked Glynis.

Lucia pointed to another prediction. "I like this one too." Glynis looked at her in disbelief. Lucia pointed to another. "This one's pretty good too. In fact, I like all of them. You know, I think all twelve signs were written exclusively for me.

"Really?" Glynis asked, intently studying the column to see if they all applied to her.

"I came to that realization years and years ago before I was accepted at the university. Then, during one of my first philosophy classes I read *On the Nature of Things* by Lucretius, the Roman poet. I remember I opened the book, and within the very first lines of the first page, it said something like *superstitions are the knowledge of the ignorant*. I concluded that day that horoscopes offer generalized suggestions about one's life that are likely to occur at some given time. These suggestions are written so that anyone can fall into believing its message is the eternal truth.

"Then later as a teacher, I chose to teach that little book. Being happily married to a physicist, I asked Gary to tell me if Lucretius's comments about the nature of the universe are true or false. To my surprise, Gary was happy to help me with my assignment because he studied Latin in college, and he had translated Lucretius's original Latin into English as one of his assignments. We went through the entire book together, and thanks to Gary, I discovered that 80 percent of its contents have real implications.

"Okay, I digress. So, speaking of horoscopes, I have also learned that the horoscope information varies from culture to culture and from generation to generation in order to seduce the reader to believe the whole thing is nothing but the truth. If you think about it, how is it possible that one column can be the same for millions and millions of people with the same sign?"

Glynis blinked blankly, struggling to comprehend. Lucia observed her young friend and thought it best to return to a semblance of common ground. She asked, "What is your sign?"

Immediately, Glynis lit up. "Pisces. March 6."

"Ah! Just like my sister Tere," Lucia observed. She reached for the newspaper and knocked over the saltshaker. Glynis gasped. Lucia set the shaker upright and smiled at Glynis.

"Aren't you, you know, going to throw some over your left shoulder?" asked Glynis.

"What good does salt all over the floor do? Does it serve any reasonable purpose? Do you know what superstitious behavior is?" Lucia asked.

"Sure, like knocking on wood or not opening an umbrella inside or crossing a black cat's path or walking under a ladder, right? My grandmother told me to be careful about them." Glynis giggled.

Lucia replied, "Those are superstitions, you are right. But superstitious behavior is . . . You know how there have been experiments to test the problem-solving abilities of pigeons? Well, picture a pigeon that has to peck a red button to get a few seeds. Next to the red button is a green button, but it delivers nothing. So the pigeon pecks the green button a couple of times and gets nothing. Then, just before it pecks the red button, it turns around twice and then pecks and *voila!* seeds drop in its cup. And the pigeon thinks, 'If I want seeds, I have to turn around twice and peck the red button. So that's what it does every time. Pecking the red button delivers the seed—it's the only thing that really works—so the turning twice is superstitious behavior. I'm sure all those things: knocking on wood and such had similar beginnings. But now, what positive result do these actions have? Grandmother's superstitions can slow your educational and emotional growth."

"I get that," Glynis said, thinking hard. "But what about Friday the thirteenth?"

Lucia laughed appreciatively. "Dear *amiga,* your Friday the thirteenth in Mexico is Tuesday the seventh, with the same spooky ideas. Speaking of Mexico where I grew up and went to school, in literature class, we read *Don Quixote de la Mancha* like you read Shakespeare. They were contemporaries, you know. Died the same day. But at any rate, Miguel de Cervantes mentioned something to the effect that the horoscopes were the common knowledge that was taking over the minds of those who were uncultured or uneducated. And as I have mentioned before, *everything is a process of cause and effect,* but horoscopes deal with effects whose causes are not necessarily there."

Glynis considered all Lucia said. She folded the newspaper and stuffed it back into her satchel. "Again you have given me very good advice, Professor, amiga. From now on, I will look at horoscopes strictly as entertaining reading, knock on wood." She rapped sharply on the table top twice.

34

Providence

A FEW DAYS later at the monthly Kat's Café gathering, Cesar came with a question for Lucia. Before she could start her talk, he asked, "What are the philosophical thoughts regarding God's will?"

"That would take ten lifetimes." Lucia laughed. "But it is an intriguing question. I'll put aside my planned topic and discuss your question."

Lucia drew a near-perfect circle on the whiteboard to its usual applause and wrote:

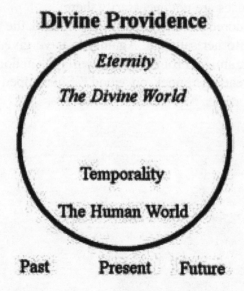

Divine Providence

Eternity

The Divine World

Temporality

The Human World

Past　　**Present**　　**Future**

"How much is up to you and how much is up to what we might call God's will?" Lucia began. "Using the philosophy of Boethius, the Roman poet of the sixth century, I will attempt to explain to you the difference between the eternal and the here and now."

"By *eternity*, we must understand the *infinite space* where minutes are not counted because there is no need for clocks in absolute present perfect with neither past nor future.

"By *temporality*, we understand the *finite space* where you and I are to see the minutes go by all the time. So if you pray to an infinite, omniscient God to give you good luck during your next interview for a new job, you must know that when you arrive at your appointment God has not really moved along with you through your past, present, and future, because an infinite, omniscient God must occupy an eternal perfect present capable of seeing all at once the entire scope of your past, present, and future.

"Now, let's assume that you were not successful in your interview because you forgot your letters of recommendation and your résumé. You ask yourself why couldn't God, who sees everything all at once, have given me a clue about my forgotten documents?

"Of course, if an omniscient God always warned you about what will happen in your future, he would automatically destroy our defining attribute: *human freedom*.

"However, you must know you can elevate your spirits in the blink of an eye and touch the eternal realm where perfect choices are made in the split second between inhaling and exhaling when you are making a conscientious choice for a better life."

Lucia scanned her audience. Uncomprehending eyes met hers. She pressed on. "Speaking of breathing, is your breathing agitated, short, accelerated, or tranquil? It is important to pay attention to your breathing because it has a direct effect on how close or how far you are to making the right choice. Our most wonderful attribute, the magnificent human freedom, is to be used but never abused. Never—not even for a second—say that you have no choice. As the existentialist philosophers like to say, we are condemned to be free, so free that the only freedom we don't have is the freedom to quit being free. But Boethius reminds us, the result of our choices is always old news in an eternal present.

Are we then ready to do everything the way our conscience dictates? Or like my mother said to me all the time, 'Lucia, what are we waiting for?' Because you are always protected by the power of the eternal infinite that covers us in a metaphysical light that shines like the most precious rainbow.

I must tell you of an experience my brother Enrique and I had while he was driving through the mountains of Spain between Seville and Madrid during a rainy but sunny day. When my brother and I saw a magnificent rainbow sitting in front of us, we couldn't help but feel awe and wonder. My brother said to me, 'I can happily die with this image in my mind.' And now, my dear friends, years later, my brother is now and forever part of the eternal present perfect."

Lucia extended her hand to Cesar, inviting him to join her before the assembled group. "Most of you know Cesar," she said. "He inspired the talk this evening." They applauded Cesar, and he shyly acknowledged their applause. Lucia turned to him. "And now, Cesar, let's keep in mind the great privilege we have, the capacity *to think before we act,* Let us embrace our freedom as we become responsible for our chosen life."

"Thank you, Professor," Cesar spoke. "Your words tonight have challenged me to be very cautious with all my choices because they now belong to me more than ever. Only God knows the outcome of the next minute. He watches me from above as I put in practice his precious gift: my *freedom of choice.*"

"Well said, my dear Cesar, well said. I see you as someone who has the knowledge of the ages that are yet to come. Congratulations, my friend!"

35

Moral or Legal

L UCIA SAT IN her favorite chair reading her own magazine
column as if she were seeing it for the first time. She smiled,
saying to herself, "There is no doubt that narcissism has wonderful
joys."

Moral or Legal

According to Immanuel Kant, the German philosopher
considered to be the most influential thinker of modern thought, the
concept of the highest, most perfect, and supreme ought not to have
condition or weakness because all these attributes belong to God.

Happiness is what we require most. Today you got up and did
whatever made you feel good in order to have tranquility of spirit,
the kind of tranquility necessary for the enjoyment of reading.
There is within you a kind of internal happiness that you learn to
cultivate. The deserved happiness is auto-constructed, which means
that throughout your day, you have acted with a sense of morality
and respect.

In philosophy, to consider oneself happy, one must be virtuous.
To be virtuous means that one does everything correctly, but not
with the kind of correctness necessary for a saint's beatitude. If we
want to be as good as the saints, we must make a lifetime of choices
full of resignation, goodness, and acceptance, always with others in
mind and never a sense of self-gain.

You may remember the story of Mother Teresa refusing to take
the one and only bed in a house she was visiting in a poor village
in India. When one of her companions protested that she had slept
on the ground the day before, Mother Teresa responded, "That was
yesterday, and today is a new day."

Have you noticed how some people do nothing but complain? Mother Teresa did not. She accepted her fate and lived each day as God's miracle. Her life, as difficult as it may have been, never disturbed her internal peace.

When life is experienced with good will in mind, even if it is extremely difficult, one can learn to live appreciating each day. Mother Teresa lived her life virtuously and full of spiritual love and civic responsibility with the qualities needed for her to become a saint, although becoming a saint was never one of her goals. If she had, it would have destroyed the natural benevolence that was a very important ingredient in granting her sainthood after her death.

In human terms, to be virtuous means to do everything guided by moral and ethical conduct. In this case, I am talking about the moral law and not the civil law. Let's go back to the happiness I described at the beginning, the kind of happiness that is earned thanks to the virtuous behavior that sometimes we lose. Why do we lose it? Because we keep forgetting how to put in practice the concept of moral virtue.

Under civil law, one can protect oneself with the aid of a lawyer who happens to be good at his craft, but not necessarily good in philosophical terms when goodness is virtuous activity. An example is the famous case of O. J. Simpson. In 1995, Simpson was acquitted of the murder of Nicole Brown Simpson and Ronald Goldman after a lengthy, internationally publicized criminal trial. The jury of twelve of his peers declared him not guilty.

I remember what I was thinking during the trial that occupied my television for an entire year. I couldn't help but think that must be enjoying happy days, a kind of a golden era, if the trial of an ex-football player could be the most important news—not just of a day, week, or month, but of an entire year. Or was the O. J. story used to cover a political reality more hidden than not? That, I personally will never know. But what I do know is that this sad case was the lawyers' success because they were clever enough to present to O. J.'s jury the *world of appearances* versus the *world of reality* with the glove found at the scene of the crime. It did not fit O. J.'s hand, but that may have been due to leather shrinking after it got wet. Remember the celebrated statement that became the legal argument? *If it does not fit, we must acquit.* And right in front of our eyes, O. J. was acquitted, thus making a very immoral crime absolutely legal.

You may also remember what happened with O. J. later in Las Vegas during his second well-known criminal trial, He ended up with a sentence of up to thirty-three years in prison, not because he had committed that horrible double murder but because the Las Vegas District Attorney prevailed in the case of armed robbery and kidnapping. Did the earlier case influence the second? Perhaps.

We must remember that when good conduct is interrupted, the road toward happiness is also severed. Do you recall a day when you called your job and pretended to be sick due to plain laziness? Instead of enjoying a great day, it became very difficult because you lied? On the other hand, a day when we have a genuine day off makes a difference, and the whole day is a kind of reward. Keep in mind that good moral choices always transcend the dimensions of one's entire life.

Let's not run the red light because no one is around and we think we can break the law and get away with it. What we really break is the continuity of well deserved happiness.

Thus, my dear reader, I wish you the best of virtuous, happy days.

36

Deficiency or Excess

PAULINE BURST IN to her professor's house, passing Sam who held the door, stepping between the girls playing a board game on the floor, and encountering Gary in the kitchen, putting away dinner dishes.

"Try her office," Gary advised.

Pauline plunged into Lucia's office, breathless.

"A philosophical emergency?" Lucia asked. "I can't imagine. Have a seat. Can I get you a glass of water?"

Soon Pauline collected herself. "Thank you for seeing me at this late hour. I'm very confused," she said.

Yes, you are, Lucia thought. "Pauline, I understand whatever it is may be very important to you at this moment. Remember how we discussed how to prioritize? How you should ask yourself if this is truly an emergency, or if you should have the patience to wait for a time that is more convenient for both of us, say, my office hours?"

Crestfallen, Pauline rose. "I'm sorry, Professor. I shouldn't have bothered you." She got up and turned to leave.

"Pauline. You're already here. Sit back down and let's talk." Lucia said.

"Okay. There's one of those emotional conflicts that I don't understand," Pauline explained. "I have three things, and I don't know if they're related. The first is Beatriz—"

"Beatriz-with-the-cookies Beatriz?"

"Uh-huh. I'm worried about her self-image. See, when Beatriz visits Louise, that makes her feel fat because Louise is like, you know, not really anorexic, but she weighs, like, ninety pounds. Then Beatriz goes to see Roberta who weighs, I don't know, three hundred or something, and that makes Beatriz feel pretty okay about herself. Professor, when I weighed with Beatriz at the gym, she only weighs 117. So, my question is, how can I help Beatriz understand that she is okay, and her weight is good and healthy?" Pauline hardly took a breath before she went on.

"I think this ties in, but I'm not sure. My Cousin Chuck's wife gets really mad at him because he drinks two beers every night. That's all. Just two. His friend drinks, like, eight or ten beers every night, but Chuck's wife says two is way too many. Chuck says that's not fair.

"Finally, this guy I've known since middle school, Raul, smokes only when he's nervous, may be two or four cigarettes a day, but he is already coughing a lot. Then his sixty-year-old uncle smokes three packs a day and goes out on Saturdays and Sundays and plays senior soccer without a hitch. What's up with that?"

Lucia thought carefully before responding. She swiveled in her desk chair. "Who has the biggest problem, do you think? Beatriz? Chuck? Raul? Why is it that we love to compare our lifestyle with our neighbors? Before I help you to understand your friends' problems, I'll tell you a story and see if it provides insight. Do you remember my neighbor Adele's nephew, my godchild, Alfonso?"

"He's the gangbanger, right? Yeah, I remember him from the news." Pauline leaned in, very interested.

"That's him. I had him in here and gave him a piece of my mind," Lucia told her, "which lasted for about a day. Alfonso and his gang hit another convenience store, and then the bodega on Fourth and then went to the north side and hit those."

"I saw that on TV," Pauline interjected.

"They would rob a store and split up the money and cigarettes and liquor, and when that ran out, they started all over again. Finally, Alfonso came to his senses and realized if he did not get out, he was going to get shot or give his poor mother a heart attack. So he came up with a plan. He and his gang robbed the Grab 'n' Go, and they all ran out, except Alfonso. He pretended to pull a muscle so he couldn't run. Then the police caught and arrested him.

"I heard about that," Pauline said.

"Fortunately for him, he was still a juvenile," Lucia said. "He got six months in jail that they reduced to eight weeks and community service. Now, he's on probation and staying away from his old cohort. I've talked to him, and he tells me that was the only way he knew how to change the course of his life. I had tried to help him, but he didn't go for it. When I told him following my advice would have saved him that time in jail, that he did not have to go to such an extreme, he just laughed. But on the other hand, Aristotle would say that what for me is Alfonso's extreme for him was his happy medium."

Lucia crooked her finger for Pauline to come close. "Tell me," she whispered conspiratorially, "have you ever taken a grape in the supermarket, just to try it?"

Pauline giggled nervously. "Who hasn't, Professor?"

"Hmmm," Lucia continued. "If I steal a single grape or a bottle of wine or several acres of a vineyard, I am a thief. I don't believe in nuance here. Stealing is stealing. You may regret what you have done and atone and make amends, but a thief who steals and does not get caught becomes as proud of his successes as if he had done the best of deeds. When this pleasure is mistaken, the thief without ethics and morals will even brag about his actions."

"You said 'without ethics and morals.' So conscience, morality, and the knowledge of things done well make a difference to the individual person, Professor?"

"Yes, Pauline! You have the right question, so you can have confidence in yourself. What we need to remember is that between *deficiency and excess* lie *moderation and temperance.* Knowing how to choose the *right thing*, at the *right time*, in the *right place*, and for the *right reason* is what gives us the feeling of self-respect. Aristotle put it eloquently when he said *"Happiness or Eudemonia is the result of an active life governed by reason."* Our obligation is to put this formula into practice, then sit back and relax and collect the happy dividends as we live a good and moral life.

Pauline only seemed dazed. Lucia had learned a while before that this was Pauline's thinking face: eyes glazed, jaw slack, tongue slightly protruding. In a moment, Pauline snapped to, smiled brightly, and said, "I got it. I know what I'm going to say to my friends to get them out of their problems."

"That's good. But remember even my best efforts failed Alfonso. Don't take it personally if your magic wand of philosophy doesn't produce the results you want for your friends," Lucia cautioned.

"All the same," Pauline beamed, getting up to leave. "You helped me clarify a direction. Thanks, and I'll see you in class. I'll see myself out, okay?"

"Pauline," Lucia said, "Try to remember about office hours. Okay?"

37

Dead or Alive

O N THIS THIRD Saturday of the month, Lucia frantically
searched her desk drawers for her passport. Not there. She
looked in her bedroom dresser drawer where she kept her scarves and
sometimes put important papers for safekeeping. Not there either.
Finally she went to her file cabinet. Found it! Filed under "passport."
Of course. Nearly everything was set for her visit to Puerto Vallarta, the
annual reunion with her siblings.

"Gary!" she called loudly, "Do you think it's okay to go ahead and
check in now online for my flight tomorrow?"

"I don't see why not!" Gary called back, busy in the kitchen.

Gary hummed in his element, the kitchen. For him, cooking combined
the tasty elements of food with the processes of physics. There in his
kitchen he addressed the epicurean questions of quantum mechanics,
preparing a table load of treats for Lucia's friends and students.

All the Kat's Café folks were due at Lucia's house for the evening.
With all she had to do for her trip, she decided to host them at her house
rather than taking the time out to go three blocks over to Kat's.

The doorbell rang. "Can somebody get that?" shouted Lucia.

"Pulling stuff out of the oven," Gary yelled back. "Can someone
open the door?"

"*Ayayay*," Lucia muttered, heading to the door. She opened it to
Beatriz, who waited there smiling broadly and holding a huge tray of
cookies. Lucia sighed.

"Beatriz, I think I told you Gary is preparing treats for tonight. Thank
you, sweetie, but I don't think we'll need those."

"It's only a few dozen," Beatriz said. "I wanted to make them.
Everybody likes them."

"Put them on the table," Lucia directed, resigned.

Gary came in with a couple of platters of empanadas and sopapillas. "What's this?" he said, seeing the center of the table taken by Beatriz's tray.

"Kind Beatriz, you know her," Lucia told him as more guests arrived.

Once the living room, dining room, and foyer filled with her group, Lucia addressed her audience.

"My dear friends, allow me to begin today by telling you that throughout the history of philosophy, we see the same questions. Some of those are "Who are we?" "Where do we come from?" "Where are we going?" Out of all the great thinkers, the one who pleases me most with the way he analyzed these questions is an Irish Bishop, George Berkeley.

"For Berkeley, God is the greatest author. Berkeley's entire philosophy can be encapsulated in one thought: *"To be is to be perceived."* For example, a table is never a table unless it is seen as a table. Someone has to perceive the table for the table to gain its presence.

"Now, let me change the theme a bit. Have you ever thought about immortality? Have you ever asked yourselves, 'Where have all those forgotten souls gone?' I say forgotten because no one, not even history, thinks of them again. Just like the table that is not a table because no one thinks of it, the same happens to all those souls that no longer exist because no one thinks of them.

"I have an older friend named Carmen. We talked one day about this precise topic. Carmen remembered how fascinating it was to be with her dad because he was such a wise man. Carmen's dad, Ignacio, was an engineer, and he always loved to read and learn. He was interested in aviation, medicine, literature, photography, history, or anything that caught his attention. He was familiar with Greek and Latin and even spoke French. Carmen told me sometimes he sang to her the *Marsellaise*.

"Carmen learned from her dad to be considerate of other people one sees on the street because each one of those people carries an entire life history. Even though we may not be able to discern the authenticity or value of others, God, through his divine mind, knows all.

"'Pay attention to those people,' her father told her. 'Look at their shoes—that will tell you how much they have walked. Pay attention to their clothes—the colors they use, the style, and the fashion will tell you who they think they are. Analyze their body language, their hands, and above all, their gestures—in them you can see the level of happiness or misery enclosed in that anonymous soul.'

"Carmen told me one day, when she was a little girl, she was in the kitchen washing the dishes. She hit a glass against the faucet and shattered it. She cried because she thought her mother would be upset because she broke the glass. But when her father found her crying, he assured her that right at that very moment someone was very glad that she broke the glass. 'Who could that be,' she wondered. 'Who would be happy I broke a glass?' Her father smiled. 'The man who makes the glasses. If no one ever broke a glass, how would that poor man earn his living?'"

Everyone laughed.

"Now, don't you feel as if you know Ignacio, Carmen's dad? Through her words, we get to understand the Ignacio that Carmen knew. Thanks to Carmen's perception of her father, it is as if we have also met him. Before beginning this chat, neither Carmen nor Ignacio had any existence because you did not know anything about them. Now through this anecdote, you may feel as if you have met both of them.

Cesar chimed in. "Do our new perceptions of these two people through your story let us participate in their divine immortality?"

"You are absolutely correct. While, according to George Berkeley, thousands and thousands of people may not be part of our lives because they are not part of our perception, it does not matter, because God has perceived them and God has given them the privilege to become immortal."

"By the way," Lucia said, "Carmen is now a little old lady. But when she speaks of her dad, she does it as if she were seeing him in front of her. For her, Ignacio is alive inside her mind. Recently I learned that she bought a one-way ticket to join her father. She is very sick, but when Carmen uses her one-way ticket to join him she will leave with a smile on her face because she believes her father's goodness means he must be very close to God.

To a chorus of sad, "Awwwws," Lucia added. "Interesting, isn't it? She may have used her ticket already, but if we ask the question: 'Are Carmen and Ignacio alive or dead?' the answer is that when we think of them, our mental perceptions keep them eternally alive. This is how each of us contributes to the immortality of all of those who have passed on. To all of those, I say, may you be lovingly remembered forever.

"Now I say good-bye to you temporarily. I take with me the perception of your presence here today. And you take the perception of my presence with you."

"Don't go, Professor, don't go," Beatriz pleaded. "Don't cash your one-way ticket."

"Mine is a round-trip ticket," Lucia said. "I'll be back in a few weeks to start next semester, Beatriz. I'm just going to visit my siblings," Lucia said giving everyone her biggest smile.

After the last student finally left, Gary asked, "What are we going to do with all these dozens of cookies? Nobody took any, even after you offered."

"We can always freeze them, my dear," she said, kissing him tenderly. "You and the kids can enjoy them while I'm gone. I'm off to Mexico."